Advance Praise

Through these devotionals, Dee enables us to face those [illegible] sion that keep us from achieving our best. He does not offer simple solutions, but rather, with profound insight into scripture and the pain of his own depression, his pastoral words become the avenue through which God speaks to us, touches us at the point of our darkness and offers the light of God's promise and Presence.

—Rev. Dr. Jack Causey
Transition Facilitator, CBF of North Carolina

Dr. Ronald "Dee" Vaughan is a practicing minister for whom I have immense respect. I have known him for twenty-five years as a fellow pastor, colleague, pastoral counselor, and friend. *Seeing in the Dark* has been helpful to me as I have dealt (and continue to deal) with losses, grief, and seasons of depression. I commend Dee's approach of offering his insights from Scripture and pastoral counseling in the form of a guidebook from a fellow pilgrim rather than a textbook on depression. I am grateful to Dee for his help and invite you to learn from him as well.

—Dr. Hardy S. Clemons
Retired Senior Pastor, First Baptist Church, Greenville, SC
Former Moderator, Cooperative Baptist Fellowship
Licensed Professional Counselor

Throughout Dee's book, he shares insights gained from both his personal journey and also his ministry to those who struggle with issues of depression.

This book is a needed personal tool that guides us in integrating our life experiences and our religious faith when experiencing times of depression that isolates us and floods us with negative thoughts about our lives. Dee's insights are valuable for those who needs support, as well as those who are supporting others during difficult times.

—Danny Garnett, D.Min.
Licensed Professional Counselor (LPC) and
Licensed Marriage and Family Therapist (LMFT)

In selecting his title, Ronald Vaughan reminds me of so many clients sitting in my counseling office over the years who struggled to find God in their depression experience. They described how their receptors for experiencing life were diminished; discovering this was also true for their connection with God . . . their receptors were diminished. I'm so grateful for this honest, practical, and hope-filled contribution to the field, helping readers to see and experience God even when we don't have the energy or native capacity to do so. I'm so glad this volume is available to address real-life needs which have been ignored for way too long.

—Rev. Mark Tidsworth
Licensed Professional Counselor
Licensed Marriage and Family Therapist
President, Pinnacle Leadership Associates

We don't know anyone who hasn't gone through a "down time" at some point in their lives. It is depressing, but fortunately this depression is short lived as we work through a problem and/or find solutions. For others of us, the depression lasts longer and a debilitating despondency steals our joy and paralyzes us. The dark cloud that hangs over us can send us into a black hole from which there seems to be no return. Dee Vaughan relates to us on all levels because he has been there . . . and back. If he were to say to you, "I feel your pain," you can believe it. He has earned the right to express that kind of empathy.

A book about depression might seem like a depressing idea unless you know Dee's style. Dee's gifts for storytelling and turn of a phrase make this collection of meditations an easy, painless journey back into the light. Through anecdotes, illustrations, examples, scripture, and prayer, the reader receives wise counsel of insight and hope that will, indeed, shine a light into a dark world.

Dee Vaughan is a master of knowing what to say, especially to those who are hurting. What a blessing *Seeing in the Dark: Biblical Meditations for People Dealing with Depression* is as a contribution to your personal preparation for allowing the dark clouds to part so that the "Son" can come shining through! Dee's comforting words soothe the soul in a way that is tender enough to gently heal a wounded spirit, yet powerful enough to lead you to a greater understanding of yourself.

—Al Walker, CSP, CPAE, Speaker, Trainer, Author
and Margaret Walker, M.Ed., NBCT Speaker, Educator, Author

Seeing *in the* Dark

Biblical Meditations *for* People Dealing *with* Depression

RONALD D. VAUGHAN

Smyth & Helwys Publishing, Inc.
6316 Peake Road
Macon, Georgia 31210-3960
1-800-747-3016

Library of Congress Cataloging-in-Publication Data

Names: Vaughan, Ronald D., author.
Title: Seeing in the dark : biblical meditations for people dealing with depression / by Ronald D. Vaughan.
Description: Macon : Smyth & Helwys, 2017. | Includes bibliographical references and index.
Identifiers: LCCN 2017025208 | ISBN 9781573129732 (pbk. : alk. paper)
Subjects: LCSH: Depression, Mental--Religious aspects--Christianity--Meditations. | Depressed persons--Religious life.
Classification: LCC BV4910.34 .V38 2017 | DDC 242/.4--dc23
LC record available at https://lccn.loc.gov/2017025208

Acknowledgments

"A cow may graze on many hills, but when she gives the milk, it is her own." I heard Dr. William Oglesby Jr. say that to a group of ministers, humorously reminding us that so much of what we have to share in preaching, writing, and counseling, we have received from others. Many times in this book, I share something with a cryptic reference like "I heard a counselor say." Though I can't remember the specific source of many things I've learned, I'm indebted to many and grateful that I've grazed on numerous good hills.

My journey toward healing began with my primary care doctor, Dr. Jim Bloodworth, who gently convinced his proud pastor patient that I needed more specialized care. Dr. Peter Owens gave me medical support during the worst days of my depression, welcomed me to collaborate with him in my treatment, and convinced his weary patient that "It's much too soon to give up." After my move to a new city, Dr. Angela Harper has continued that same quality of personal care. Charlie White and Gayle Hickman are therapists who helped me learn that healing was not only about finding the right medicine, but about understanding how I was living my life. Their fingerprints are on many pages of this book.

I didn't know how to give voice to what I'd learned about depression until I tried to help others dealing with the same darkness. I owe a great debt to the men and women who have trusted me enough to share their pain with me as their pastor and counselor. Many of this book's ideas were hammered out in the work we did together.

I wish my wife, Linda, hadn't had to live with a depressed husband or my children, Elizabeth, Josh, and Andrew, with an emotionally exhausted father, but I'm proud of how they loved me through the darkness and back into the light of life.

—Ronald D. Vaughan

Also by Ronald D. Vaughan

The Stories of My Life

To those I've followed and those I've led

in the darkness of depression;

brave souls with whom I've sought, shared,

and celebrated heavenly light.

Contents

Part IV: As You Think in Your Heart

Part V: Put Them into Practice

Part VI: Strengthen Your Brothers and Sisters

Introduction

Does the Bible say anything about depression?

In more than three decades of serving as a local church pastor, I've been asked that question a number of times. I've learned that this is not a *study* question for most people who ask it; it is more of a *survival* question. Many people who deeply love and trust God go through seasons of depression. When they do, they hunger for spiritual strength and guidance from the Scriptures. Most of them don't know where to find it.

This question became intensely personal for me almost a decade ago when I suffered with major depression. Though I had preached and taught the Bible in the churches I served, in college classrooms, and through Bible study resources I'd written for my denomination, I struggled to find the passages that could offer me the help and hope I so desperately needed. Out of this feeling of spiritual suffocation, I decided that when I discovered a biblical text and truth that enlightened, encouraged, challenged, or comforted me in my battle with emotional pain, I would write it down in a journal so I would remember it and return to it often. I hoped that, in better days, I would be able to share these discoveries with others facing the same kind of struggle.

With this mission in mind, the Scriptures spoke to me in some amazing ways and at some surprising times. One Sunday evening, I was preaching a message based on Psalm 139 and read the words, "If I say, 'Surely the darkness will hide me and the light become night around me,' even the darkness will not be dark to you; the night will shine like the day, for darkness is as light to you" (Ps 139:11-12). In the middle of that message, in the very process of preaching, a truth leapt out of the Scripture that was a gift of insight and hope: *God can see in the dark.* God can see what I can't see when I'm struggling to find my way through the dark valley of depression.

When that worship service ended, I marked those verses in my Bible and scribbled down the truth that had strengthened me. You'll recognize that Scripture and the lesson it taught me in the first devotional of this book. In fact, that passage inspired the title of this collection: *Seeing in the Dark.* I hope this collection of Scriptures and devotional thoughts will give you moments of enlightenment while you wrestle with the darkness of depression.

Let me suggest that you not read too much of this book at one time. I think these devotionals are of the most value when you spend time with one of them each day over a period of weeks. I kept each devotional fairly short because depressed people lack the energy or focus to read and retain long treatises. Remembering how things sink slowly into a depressed mind, you may want to read a single devotional several times to grasp its message and apply it to your life more fully.

Each devotional includes a suggested prayer. Let these words begin your conversation with God about what you've read and learned. Prayer was very difficult for me during my worst days of depression. If that's true for you, allow the suggested prayer to "prime the pump" and get your prayer started.

The final portion of each devotional is a truth to affirm. This closing statement boils the primary truth of the devotional down to a few words that, hopefully, will be easy to remember and share.

This book is not intended to be a cure for your depression. Most people who suffer with this illness need several sources of help. A good doctor, the right medication, and personal work with a counselor are often necessary ingredients in the healing process. I believe that the insights of the Scriptures are another source of help and hope that you need to add to your daily life as you seek greater health and wholeness.

If God uses these devotionals to shine some light into the darkness of your depression, then my prayer will be answered and I will know this book was more than worth the work.

— Dr. Ronald "Dee" Vaughan

Part I

God Can See *in the* Dark

If I say, "Surely the darkness will hide me and the light become night around me," even the darkness will not be dark to you; the night will shine like the day, for darkness is as light to you.

Psalm 139:11-12

1

God Can See in the Dark

If I say, "Surely the darkness will hide me and the light become night around me," even the darkness will not be dark to you; the night will shine like the day, for darkness is as light to you.

Psalm 139:11-12

I can't see in the dark. It's a fact of life. I've proven it many times, getting up in the night, foolishly believing I can navigate through the house without turning on a light, and then tripping over a sleeping dog, a briefcase left in the middle of the hallway so it couldn't be forgotten the next morning, or a vacuum cleaner hose someone forgot to put up after cleaning. I've literally fallen on my face because I underestimated what an enemy darkness can be.

I can't see in emotional darkness either. Emotional darkness is a pretty good description of depression. The realities of my world don't change when depression darkens my vision, but I'm changed because I can't see what I need to see to navigate through life.

In the darkness, I can't see the goodness of life. Even when I strain my brain to remember how blessed I am, I don't see it. I count my blessings but don't experience them.

In the darkness, I can't see the love of others. I'm surrounded by very loving family, friends, and coworkers, but when the darkness comes, I don't feel loved or lovable.

In the darkness, I can't see any good in myself. I may do good things and continue to do the things I normally do pretty well, but I don't give myself any credit for it, no recognition of the value of who I am or what I do. Instead, I become my own worst critic, castigating and condemning my every action and every motive behind it. In the darkness, I feel absolutely worthless.

In the darkness, I can't see God. I don't claim to have literal visions of God on good days, but I do have a sense of God's presence and see God's fingerprints on many circumstances and relationships. When the darkness comes, though, God seems far away and I feel like an abandoned child. Worship becomes a pointless routine and prayer is like calling a disconnected telephone number.

The good news for me and every person who has awakened in the deep darkness of depression is that God *can* see in the dark. God's view of me and my life are not changed by the darkness that surrounds me when depression comes.

God sees my worth as his beloved child. His promises that nothing can separate me from his love and that no one can take me out of my Father's hand are no less true when I can't see love. Even in the darkness, God loves me with an everlasting love. He sees clearly that I am his creation, his masterpiece, fearfully and wonderfully made.

Even in the darkness, God sees the plans he has for me, the future he wants me to press on toward. I may be blind to any purpose or meaning in my life, but God still sees the big picture of my calling and my hope.

God sees people who care about me and can help me move through the darkness to brighter, better days. I believe God sends those people to me when I need them and keeps knocking at the door of my darkened heart, urging me to let them in. Good friends, skilled doctors, gifted counselors, and faithful family are all around me. I may need the motivational transfusion of some tough love to convince me to let them inside my dark world to help, but God knows they are there. He put them there.

Perhaps most precious to me, God sees the other side of the valley. Depression is one of those deadly dark shadows many of us must travel through. Inside that shadow, the entire world seems darker than night with no stars to guide the journey. But God is bigger than life's valleys and all the shadows they hold. He knows that life on the other side of depression is ahead and that, amazingly, the darkness can, in time, sharpen my vision to see his work, his love, and his purpose.

Depression is a time of terrifying darkness for those in its grip, but not for the God who holds the whole world, the bright side and the dark side, in his hands. God can see in the dark. He sees you now. He hasn't lost you. And God loves you, right where you are.

Prayer

O God, I'm stumbling in the darkness. I feel lost in a strange new place. Whisper to me the good news that you see what I can't see right now. Touch my eyes and open them one day to see again life's goodness and your glory. Until then, I trust you to keep watch over my life, my worth, and my hope. Amen.

Truth to Affirm

God can see what I can't see in the darkness of depression.

2

God Is Greater than Our Hearts

There is a sure way for us to know that we belong to the truth. Even though our inner thoughts may condemn us *with storms of guilt and constant reminders of our failures*, we can know in our hearts that in His presence God Himself is greater than any accusation. He knows all things.

1 John 3:19-20, *The Voice*

I once owned a car with a broken gas gauge. When the tank was empty, the needle pointed to "E." When the tank was half full, the gauge still read empty. When the gas tank was filled to overflowing, the needle budged just a little, moving slightly to the right of the empty mark. No matter how much fuel was in that car's tank, the gauge gave me the same message, "Your tank is empty."

Because the gauge was not a reliable indicator of how much fuel was in my gas tank, I learned to disregard its message. I also devised another way to assess how much fuel was in the tank. I found a long stick I could slide through the nozzle into the tank, then pull it out to see how much of the stick was wet with gasoline. You could call it a literal dipstick for my gas tank. It wasn't fancy or stylish, but it worked, telling me the truth despite the false message of a broken gauge.

Human emotions are a kind of gauge of the heart, an indicator of the fullness or emptiness of our lives and relationships. When feelings are working well, they help us experience life fully and warn us when some aspect of our lives is running low. The problem with feelings is that they are a gauge that sometimes breaks. When you are in a season of depression, your feelings can give you the wrong feedback. Like my broken gas gauge, feelings hijacked by depression can give you a constant message of emptiness. You may read that flawed feeling in various ways:

My life is a total wreck.
No one loves or respects me.
I am a complete failure.
I cannot be right with God and feel this way.

What do you do when you realize that your emotional gauges are broken? First, you must learn to question the meaning of what you feel. When you know your emotions are depressed, you must fight the tendency to accept that empty feeling as an accurate appraisal of your life. Second, you must find another way to measure the fullness or emptiness of your life, a kind of emotional and spiritual dipstick to help you work around feelings that aren't giving you a true reading. The letter of 1 John offers you and me a tool that can help us get beyond our broken emotional gauges.

God is greater than our hearts. What God says about who we are and our standing with him is a faithful measure of the truth. God knows everything about why our feelings are giving us false messages. He also knows that his love for us and faithfulness to us do not depend on our feelings.

This passage also means that God is a higher authority than our hearts in determining where we stand with him. When feelings are broken, we may feel far from God, unable to pray, far short of the purpose we believe God has for our lives. But our feelings are not the final authority. They do not have the last word. God is greater than our hearts. We are who God says we are, no matter what we feel.

Prayer

Loving Father, my feelings are so broken right now. They tell me I'm far from you and useless to the people around me. Teach me that you are greater than my heart. Help me to trust your word and your promises about who I am as your beloved child. Amen.

Truth to Affirm

God is greater than my heart.

3

A Feast in the Presence of My Enemies

You prepare a table before me in the presence of my enemies.
You anoint my head with oil; my cup overflows.

Psalm 23:5

Depression sufferers live in the presence of enemies. Physical symptoms make your body hurt. Sickened thoughts assume the worst about you and what others think about you. A lack of motivation makes the first step of even the best actions feel impossible. The future looks blank as hoping and planning are shrouded in darkness. Those who fight against depression face formidable foes, to be sure. Even when these enemies are not actively attacking the goodness of your life, you know they exist and that they might attack at any time.

How can you live joyfully when you know your emotional enemies are always present? Psalm 23 is a masterpiece picture of who God is, how God loves, and the life those who belong to God enjoy. In verse 5, the psalmist praises God for welcoming him to a great feast. God, the gracious host, prepares a table for his cherished guest, a table covered with an abundance of food. This is a beautiful picture of God's provision, but that is not the most life-changing truth this verse expresses. This verse affirms God's protection of those who feast at his table.

When a Middle Eastern host welcomed a guest to his table, he promised that guest his full protection while he was there. Any attack on a guest would be considered an attack on the host as well. Though the sojourner was fully aware his enemies were nearby, he could enjoy the good things his host provided because his host promised his protection.

God invites you to his table. God, the gracious host, wants you to be his guest. He wants you to enjoy the best things he has to offer. And he gives you this amazing invitation at the very time and place your enemies are present. God doesn't suddenly run every enemy away from your life. Those who fight depression will face many battles on many days. But he does promise you that, in spite of your enemies, you can be fed. You can be nourished. You can enjoy life's good things. You can share God's feast in the presence of your enemies.

Prayer

Gracious Host, I realize I'm starving myself to death waiting for my enemies to leave my life. I need to accept your invitation. I need to take my seat at your table. I need to trust your promise of protection and rest in the truth that I can enjoy a feast of life's blessings, even when I see my enemies nearby. I'll face them again, but not with an empty heart. Feed me. Fill me. Strengthen me to win. Amen.

Truth to Affirm

I can feast on God's grace and life's goodness,
even in the presence of my enemies.

4

God Speaks Out of the Storm

Then out of the storm the LORD spoke to Job.

Job 38:1, *Good News Translation*

I've learned the most in the classes I didn't want to take. That was true in my college and seminary days. It's also been true for me in the school of life. One of my least wanted but most life-changing classes was my depression. Some of my lessons were factual. I now know a great deal more about medicines, exercise, journaling, and nutrition. But the most valuable truths I gained in my least-wanted class were profoundly personal.

At the most dramatic moment of the story of Job, God speaks to Job out of a storm. Job hears God's voice and experiences God's power and sovereignty in a much more personal way than ever before. Having heard God speak to him through the storm, Job trades a secondhand faith of what others have told and taught him for a firsthand faith growing out of his own experience of God's power and presence in the midst of suffering. He confesses, "My ears had heard of you but now my eyes have seen you" (Job 42:5).

In my own storm of depression, God spoke. What I learned is written on every page of this book, but I will name a few life-changing revelations here.

- I learned to practice more of what I'd long been preaching. I had to go beyond telling others how to live more fully to taking careful inventory of my own life and rebuilding my own health and happiness.

- I learned that asking for help is not a sign of weakness but an honest recognition of my humanity and an expression of faith that God will use many means to meet my needs and restore my soul.
- I learned that my ministry can become not only an opportunity to serve but also a temptation to hide my needs and struggles from others—and even from myself. I realized that God never calls me by a title; God only calls me by my name.
- I saw the vast difference between those who, in genuine friendship, love at all times and those who are no more than friendly strangers who won't be inconvenienced by anyone else's pain.
- Spiritual warfare changed from a theological idea to a daily personal battle as life and death fought hand-to-hand in the trenches of my soul.
- Grace was no longer simply a key concept in my interpretation of the Christian gospel. It became a *lifeline* that held me up when every claim to self-sufficiency had sunk and disappeared beneath the waves of my storm.
- I learned that I really can come to God, in the words of the hymn, "just as I am," and find a welcome, an embrace, a cleansing, and a home.

No, I didn't want to take this class called depression. But still I am thankful that God speaks out of life's storms. In the midst of your storm, may you hear God speak and, through that experience, may you know God and his love more personally and more powerfully than ever before.

Prayer

Almighty God, you know I don't want this storm and don't like it.
But if I must pass through it, please speak to me as you did to Job.
This pain is too costly to waste. In this storm, may I come to know you,
not just know about you. In this storm, may I learn that
your grace truly is enough for me. Amen.

Truth to Affirm

God speaks to me in my storms.

5

Pain Can Give Birth to New Life

"I will not cause pain without allowing something new to be born," says the LORD.

Isaiah 66:9, *NCV*

The day my first grandchild, Liam, was born, Linda and I arrived at the hospital and went to my daughter Elizabeth's room to spend time with her and her husband, Josh. Every two or three minutes, Elizabeth would have a contraction, a passing moment of tension and discomfort, but between those contractions, she shared conversation with us, posed for pictures, and even joked about becoming a mother. But in a few hours, the pain she was feeling became far more intense and came more often. I saw suffering written on her face and the fear that comes from hurting like you've never hurt before. The time came for all "nonessential personnel" to exit the room, leaving Elizabeth with her husband, her nurse, and the challenge of enduring the pain she was feeling.

As excited as I was about becoming a grandfather, I spent the next several hours pacing up and down hallways, interrogating anyone who came out of Elizabeth's room, and even putting my ear up against the hospital room door to hear any clue that could tell me how my girl was holding up in her battle with pain. A few times, a doctor or nurse caught me listening at the doorway, but I didn't care. I was worried about my daughter. Everything inside me wanted her pain to end. For hours, we heard the voices of doctors and nurses coaching her. We heard her cries of anguish as she fought the good fight. Then, at 7:21 p.m., almost fourteen hours after her labor had begun, my daughter's pain turned to the joy of a new life. Outside in the hallway, we who had been listening to Elizabeth's struggle heard something new, a little voice crying out to announce his entrance into the world. I hugged Linda and we remembered three such days in our own marriage. But now we felt the joy of our daughter's pain leading to the miracle of a new life.

Childbirth is one of the most painful and dangerous experiences a woman can endure. I wish it were different. I wished it a hundred times that night. But, in God's plan, pain is the price of new life. It's true for a woman giving birth. It's also true for any person struggling through the dark night of depression.

Liam's birth taught me that, for any of us, pain is the price of new life. So many people long for some kind of new beginning: deeper faith, greater faithfulness, victory over a struggle, joy on the other side of weeping. But what we must realize is that we won't experience the miracle of new life unless we are willing to endure the pain that new life demands. New life demands the pain of honesty, confession, heartbroken repentance, letting go of the old in order to make room for the new, enduring a night of darkness in order to see the glory of a new day.

The Apostle Paul tells the Galatians that he is bearing great pain for the purpose of seeing Christ more alive in their hearts and in their church. He writes, in Galatians 4:19, "My dear children, for whom I am again in the pains of childbirth until Christ is formed in you . . . ."

So many times in my battle with depression, I've asked God why I've hurt so badly—why the people I love have hurt so badly. I don't think I'll ever fully understand the *reason* for this pain, not on this side of heaven, but I can find hope in the *result* of this pain. Depression can be the labor pains of a new life. New insights can be realized. New skills can be learned. New wisdom can be gained. A healthier, happier lifestyle can be built and followed. By God's grace and power, my pain and your pain can be the beginning of a new life.

Prayer

God, some days all I feel is pain, and I want the pain to stop. Help me see that my pain may, by your grace, be the labor pains of a better life. You are great enough to work even depression to my good. Strengthen my trust in you and my willingness to follow where you lead—through this night of hurting to the dawn of a new life. Amen.

Truth to Affirm

Depression can be the labor pains of a new and more abundant life.

6

No Condemnation

Therefore, there is now no condemnation for those who are in Christ Jesus, because through Christ Jesus the law of the Spirit of life set me free from the law of sin and death.

Romans 8:1-2

One of the most life-draining, defeating symptoms of my depression was a constant internal voice of condemnation. I didn't literally hear a voice, but its message would not have been any clearer or more caustic if I'd heard it with my ears. Nothing I did was good enough. The internal messages claimed that no one around me cared if I lived or died. The people with whom I worked and even my family would be far better off without me, I heard again and again.

My heart was so saturated with condemnation that when I opened my mouth to speak, judgment and blame spewed out on everyone else. I sometimes felt like a ventriloquist's dummy speaking someone else's words with someone else's voice. Most of the wounds caused by the vitriolic words I spoke in those days have healed, but some have left scars that, sadly, will always be part of my relationships with others.

How do you find freedom from the cacophony of condemnation? You can't unplug it as you would an annoying stereo or sound system. My first step in confronting and overcoming those condemning messages was to believe the promise Paul makes to the Romans and to us: "Therefore, there is now no condemnation for those who are in Christ Jesus . . . ." God's message to me is that I am not condemned. Quite the contrary, I am the redeemed, secure, beloved child of God. When I hear messages of condemnation, they are not from God. Sickness is speaking. Pain is crying out. Frustration and fatigue are tempted to give up. Depression has taken over the conversation and will not shut up.

Once I know that messages of condemnation are not from God, I can confront them as the lies they are. I can also claim the courage to share those morbid messages with people I trust, getting them out into the light and warmth of a caring relationship, where people who hear God more clearly can help me sort out reality from distortion and truth from falsehood. Many of the coldest condemning words melt like snowflakes on a sun-warmed road when spoken in the presence of a loving friend.

God does not condemn his children. Once you know that great truth, you can use it to measure every message that crosses your mind. As Paul wrote to the Romans earlier in that letter, "Let us think of God as true, even if every living man be proved a liar" (Rom 3:4b, Phillips).

Trust God and question the wounded ears of your heart.

Prayer

O God, amid the clamor of the crowd of condemning voices I hear within me, I long to hear your voice, your truth, your forever love. Help me trust your promises that I may stand strong against depression's lies and welcome others into my battle for truth. Amen.

Truth to Affirm

No matter what your heart is hearing, God is not condemning you.

7

With All Your Heart

You will seek me and find me when you seek me
with all your heart.

Jeremiah 29:13

Good counselors ask good questions. The counselor who helped me work through my season of depression once asked me a question that revealed a source of my pain and a path I needed to take toward healing. She asked, "Who knows your whole story?"

"Whole story?" I replied, not because I didn't understand the question but because I wasn't sure how I would answer.

"Yes, your whole story. Who knows everything about what's happening in your life?"

After a moment of silent soul-searching, my honest answer, which felt more like a confession, was "No one." Not my colleagues, not my friends, not my brother or sister, not even my wife knew everything about the struggle I was facing. Answering that one question revealed to me one significant source of my depression.

Though I affirm the belief that God is omniscient—that God knows everything—in one important way, God didn't know my whole story either. God didn't know in the sense that I hadn't brought my struggle to him in honest prayer and offered it to him to be illumined by his truth and transformed by his grace. Part of my heart, the part that was most wounded, was private property. No one was allowed there but me.

I was doing to God what I'd been doing to my church. For many weeks, I put on a good front, answered the bell when the time came to lead another worship service or wedding or funeral or committee meeting, but I was careful not to disclose the part of me that was dying more than living.

I had been giving God a performance but not my heart—at least not my whole heart.

When I hear the challenge to do something "with your whole heart," I first think of it as a call to give greater effort to what I want to achieve. This is not what Jeremiah means when he calls us to seek God with all our hearts. Jeremiah is calling us not to greater effort but to greater honesty. If you and I want to find God in our struggle with depression, we must bring everything in our hearts to him for hearing and for healing. We can't pray and hide at the same time, not when facing such a deep wound and urgent need.

Finding God in the battle of depression begins with coming to God in the spirit of the old hymn, "Just as I Am." I have to seek God with all my heart, everything that is in my heart, if I want God to guide me in finding the road that leads from where I truly am to where I long to be.

Prayer

God of truth, I struggle to bring all that is in my heart to you. You are holy, and so many of the thoughts and feelings I have right now seem so wrong. Teach me that the only way to find you is, as Jesus said, in spirit and in truth. I trust your love for me enough to give you my whole heart, everything that is in my heart, so you can begin to make it new. Amen.

Truth to Affirm

Healing from depression demands the honesty and courage to give God everything that is in my heart.

8

Seeing God through Dark Glass

We are confident that God is able to orchestrate everything to work toward something good *and beautiful* when we love Him and accept His invitation to live according to His plan.

Romans 8:28, *The Voice*

The stained-glass windows of our church sanctuary were being repaired and restored. Several times a day, I couldn't resist leaving my office and walking to the sanctuary to see how the work was progressing. When I asked one of the workmen how his day was going, he said, "I want to show you something. I just finished a piece of glass that needed to be replaced in one of your windows." I followed him with great excitement to where he'd been shaping and staining the glass. As we walked, I imaged a piece of glass in fiery red or rich blue or regal purple to be added to one of the windows. We arrived at his workbench, where he unwrapped a piece of glass about the size of my palm. He held it up and said, "Here it is. I've finally gotten it just right." When I saw what he had made, I wondered how he could be so excited about it. It was dark. The bottom was black as night. The top was smoky with dark black streaks. I frankly saw nothing beautiful about it. I don't know if he read my reaction (I don't hide my feelings very well), but he seemed to understand that I didn't yet see the value of what he'd made. He walked me back to the window where this piece of glass would be installed. He held it in place, alongside scores of other pieces of many colors. Only then did I see what I couldn't see in the single piece of glass. That dark smoky glass was as important to the window and the story it told as were the brightest colors. The artist needed the dark pieces as well as the bright ones to create such a beautiful picture and symbolize the story of Jesus as our Good Shepherd.

Some seasons of my life, when seen by themselves, have been like dark pieces of glass—murky moments that seem to have no redemptive purpose or meaning. Depression has surely been among the darkest of those times. Looking at that part of my life alone, I had to say to God,

Why does this part of my life look like this?
It's so dark.
It's ugly.
The light can't shine through it.
How could you, my loving Heavenly Father, allow a piece of my life to be shaped and stained like this?

In such times, when the darkness is all I see, I need God to take that dark piece of my journey and show me again the whole picture of my life. With grace to see the bigger picture, the dark times can become part of the story my life needs to tell.

- The times when I was weak but he was strong.
- The times when I wandered but he found me and brought me home.
- The times when I learned that his grace really is enough.
- The times when only a living Savior could change my sorrow into joy.

In your life and in mine, God knows what the artists who make stained-glass windows know; all the colors, the dark and the bright, can work together to make a more beautiful, more complete picture of a life spent loving and living for God.

Prayer

Father, I struggle to see beauty in this dark part of my life. Help me see, or at least help me trust you until I can see, the bigger picture you are creating. Many pieces are beautiful and radiant. The dark ones are part of the picture of my life too, and they represent some of the times when I've seen your power most at work. I trust you to complete the picture of my life story and to make it beautiful. Amen.

Truth to Affirm

This dark piece of my life can become part of the beautiful picture God is creating.

9

The Potter's Wheel Is Still Turning

So I went down to the potter's house, and I saw him working at the wheel. But the pot he was shaping from the clay was marred in his hands; so the potter formed it into another pot, shaping it as seemed best to him. Then the word of the LORD came to me: "O house of Israel, can I not do with you as this potter does?" declares the LORD. "Like clay in the hand of the potter, so are you in my hand, O house of Israel."

Jeremiah 18:3-6

God told Jeremiah to go the potter's house because, through the work of the potter, God would reveal his message to Jeremiah. The prophet watched as the potter worked at the wheel, purposefully shaping the clay with a beautiful and useful end in mind. But, as the potter worked, something went wrong. The clay was "marred in his hands." The clay wasn't responding to the potter's touch the way he intended. It was falling short of the purpose the potter had for it.

At this point, I believe, Jeremiah saw the heart of the message God wanted him to grasp. The potter didn't throw the clay away. He didn't reject it as useless. The potter continued to work on the clay. He worked with an unrelenting purpose to create a beautiful, useful vessel. Even when the clay was marred, when the journey toward fulfillment was delayed, the potter's wheel continued to turn.

God tells Jeremiah that God's people are like clay in his hands. God works with a purpose to bring his dream for his people into reality. To make that truth personal, God is at work in your life and mine with divine purpose. He works to make our lives reflect his beauty and glory, to make our lives useful vessels for his kingdom's work.

Then something goes wrong. For some reason our lives aren't taking shape. Despite the work of God the Potter, the dream isn't coming true. Many things can mar a vessel, but depression is certainly one of them. Depression can leave you feeling like a flawed, unfinished divine project. Feeling marred, falling short of the dream, you may believe that your life is over.

Have the courage and hope to see what Jeremiah saw long ago and apply it to your life today. The Potter's wheel is still turning. His hands are still upon you, shaping your life despite your flaws and your struggles, with the goal of revealing his glory through you. You need not give up on your life, because God hasn't given up. He does some of his best work with vessels that need an extra touch, another try, a new beginning.

If you feel like giving up because of the struggles you face, look up and see. The Potter's wheel is still turning.

Prayer

Heavenly Potter, I feel like a marred vessel. Depression seems to have taken away so much promise and potential from my life. I've despaired that your work in me has failed. I need to see what Jeremiah saw long ago. I need to see you at work with flawed people like me. I need to know you haven't surrendered your dream for my life. Your hand is upon me. Your purpose is shaping me. I praise you that your potter's wheel is still turning. Amen.

Truth to Affirm

The Potter's wheel is still turning, making something beautiful and useful of my life.

Part II

Choosing *Life*

This day I call heaven and earth as witnesses against you that I have set before you life and death, blessings and curses. Now choose life, so that you and your children may live and that you may love the LORD your God, listen to his voice, and hold fast to him.

Deuteronomy 30:19-20a

10

Choose Life

This day I call heaven and earth as witnesses against you that I have set before you life and death, blessings and curses. Now choose life, so that you and your children may live and that you may love the LORD your God, listen to his voice, and hold fast to him.

Deuteronomy 30:19-20a

Life is lost or found in the choices you make. The book of Deuteronomy confronts God's people with the importance of making wise choices and the life-giving or life-destroying consequences our choices create. The people are told they can choose to love and honor God and experience life in its fullness. They can also choose to forget God, live as they please, and die.

Those who struggle with depression often feel powerless in the presence of an illness that seems to hold every aspect of their lives hostage. We must realize depression doesn't take away our power to choose. Our choices will move us toward a fuller life or toward death. The warning is sobering. The choices we make can sink us deeper into the quicksand of depression. But the hope of this passage is encouraging and empowering. We can, even in the dark valley of depression, make choices that move us toward healing and health.

You choose life . . .

. . . when you admit your struggles and stop denying them.

. . . when you seek and accept the help you need.

. . . when you do the right thing even though you don't feel like doing anything.

. . . when you reach out to people instead of withdrawing from everyone.

. . . when you forgive those who've hurt you, realizing that this choice is a greater gift to you than anyone else.
. . . when you challenge your negative, self-condemning thoughts and practice thinking in new, life-affirming ways.
. . . when you take responsibility for your own life, your thoughts, your feelings, and your actions, and insist that others do the same.
. . . when you say "no" to unfair expectations.
. . . when you express what is truly in your heart.
. . . when you stop trying to fix other people.
. . . when you know that God is greater than your heart and that, no matter what you feel, God can be trusted to hold you and your destiny in his hand.
. . . when you dare to believe that after a long, dark night of weeping, joy will come in the morning.

Depression can end in life or death. You walk toward one or the other one choice at a time. The good news is that you *can* choose life.

Prayer

Lord, I didn't choose to be in this dark valley, but I'm beginning to see that I need to make good choices to get out of it. I feel so powerless over my depression. Help me claim my power to choose, let go of lies and burdens, and open my life to truth and strength and joy. Through the choices I can make today, help me move just a small step closer to abundant life. Amen.

Truth to Affirm

The choices I make can make me more fully alive.

11

When I Kept Silent

When I kept silent, my bones wasted away through my groaning all day long.

Psalm 32:3

We are as sick as we are secret.

I don't know who first put that big truth into so few words. I've heard several teachers and counselors repeat it and put its insight to good use. Silence is a terrible adversary of those wrestling with depression.

Silence is isolating. Depressed people tend to withdraw from others, starving their need for community and support. When those who are depressed keep their struggles a secret, they place yet another barrier between themselves and people who can help.

Silence suffocates hope. The act of sharing our struggles is an expression of hope, showing that we believe another person can understand and that the very process of verbalizing our emotional battles may bring new insights into how healing can begin. Silence suffocates that hope. Sharing brings hope to life.

Silence surrenders to sickness. One of the most needed weapons in the battle with depression is a sense of "personal agency," the confidence that I can act upon my life and make a positive difference. Silence surrenders that power and leaves feelings of helplessness. Talking about steps toward healing makes them more real. Committing to lifestyle changes out loud to a friend creates accountability and invites support. Sharing welcomes allies into the battle.

Rediscover your voice. Find a person and a place where you can share your struggles and seek direction in the journey of healing. You may have a trusted friend who can help. Your minister may have strong counseling gifts. You may need a therapist who can offer you a trained ear and an informed view of your life and your choices.

You are as sick as your struggle is secret. Speak up for your life.

Prayer

God of courage, I confess that I've been afraid to talk about my sickness. I've feared that people might think I'm crazy or a problem person to be avoided. I also see that sharing my struggle with someone who cares will reveal helpful steps that I don't yet realize I need to take. Oh God, I cry out to you. I believe you hear my prayer. I know the difference confessing my pain makes. Guide me to the people in whose presence I can find my voice and speak up for my life. Amen.

Truth to Affirm

I am as sick as I am secret, so I will speak up for my life.

12

Naming Our Demons

Then Jesus asked him, "What is your name?"
"My name is Legion," he replied, "for we are many."

Mark 5:9

In the ancient world, people believed that knowing a person's name gave them a degree of power over that person. You might use your knowledge of someone's name to give the person a blessing or place a curse on him or her. This is why, in some biblical stories, the characters are reticent to reveal their names. A name was more than a label. Often a name was chosen to describe the essence of a person's life. When you knew a name, you often knew something about the nature, the character, the spirit of a person. The knowledge revealed by a name gave you power.

In Mark 5, Jesus encounters a man controlled and tormented by evil. Before Jesus heals the man from the malignant power that has taken possession of his life, Jesus asks a question: "What is your name?" Jesus wanted to hear the name of the man's struggle before he set this struggler free. Jesus learned the name of the man's demon before he threw it out.

I have heard counselors say, "Nothing changes until it becomes what it is." Naming our demons is part of the healing journey for those who suffer with depression. No, I do not believe that depression is literally an evil spirit that possesses a human life, but I do believe that naming the sources of our pain and problems is an essential step in finding freedom from them.

Naming is confessing. The old gospel song says, "It's me, O Lord, standing in the need of prayer." In the journey of healing, we must give up our pretensions of being self-sufficient and our denial of problems, which are so obvious to others, and be honest about our needs. Naming our demons positions us to receive the help we need.

Naming is focusing. Depression says, "You are a worthless, unlovable person whose life is a total wreck." Naming the sources of our pain and problems gives us new perspective. Focusing on a source of pain allows us to say, "You are a good person, loved infinitely by God and cared for by others, who has a problem to be addressed, a wound to be healed. Your life and the goodness of your life are bigger than your depression." Naming our demons helps us focus on what hurts and separate it from the goodness of the rest of our lives.

Naming is sharing. Talking about our emotional wounds gets them out of dark places of hiding into the warmth and light of a caring relationship. What sometimes seems unconquerable in secret becomes a winnable war in the presence of an understanding helper.

Naming is empowering. Depression feels like a dark, mystical, larger-than-life force that the sufferer cannot clearly identify, much less defeat. Learning the true name of the struggle—lifestyle, chemical imbalance, depressive thinking, childhood trauma, codependent relationship, etc.—gives the hurt an identity and boundaries, a target at which therapy can be aimed, a specific finite challenge that can be overcome.

Naming is freeing. Keeping emotional secrets is preoccupying and exhausting. Naming our demons sets us free from that pointless, smothering task, freeing wasted energy for the work of learning, growing, and healing. Naming our struggles also frees us from the lie that if people knew our struggles, they would not love us. The people who walk away from you because you're depressed never loved you. The people who love you won't walk away when you name your demons.

Naming our demons, the sources of our depression, is a critical step in throwing them out.

Prayer

God, nothing is hidden from you. I've wasted time pretending I'm not in pain. I've given my depression more power over me than it deserves by keeping it a secret. Give me the courage to be honest with you, knowing you are big enough and loving enough to hear any question, any pain, any complaint, even cries of despair. Guide me to the people with whom I can name my demons, the people in whose presence I can find help and hope. I claim the power of naming my pain. Use that power to heal me. Amen.

Truth to Affirm

Naming my demons will help me throw them out.

13

Change Requires Action

Therefore everyone who hears these words of mine and puts them into practice is like a wise man who built his house on the rock. The rain came down, the streams rose, and the winds blew and beat against that house; yet it did not fall, because it had its foundation on the rock. But everyone who hears these words of mine and does not put them into practice is like a foolish man who built his house on sand. The rain came down, the streams rose, and the winds blew and beat against that house, and it fell with a great crash.

Matthew 7:24-27

Jesus defines wisdom as hearing his words and putting them into practice. The essence of foolishness, he says, is hearing what he teaches but doing nothing about it. People who struggle with depression must realize that change requires action. Reading books, listening to sermons, or hearing the insights of a gifted counselor won't do much to restore your health unless you use what you hear to change how you live each day. I've known many people who confused showing up for regular counseling sessions with taking the daily action demanded to get better. These folks must be related to those who mistake sitting in church once a week for living the Christian life.

The counselor who helped me the most in my depression work gave me homework—written, thought-provoking, new-habit-forming homework. "Let me see what you've done since our last conversation" was a courteous way of holding me accountable for doing the daily work of exploring and establishing new ways of thinking and acting.

What makes this call to action even more urgent is how difficult taking action is for depressed people. Depression often causes a lack of energy, initiative, and motivation. Doing nothing or delaying action is never easier than when depression saps your physical and emotional strength.

Let me offer you one specific bit of advice that helped me be honest with myself about when I was putting my life lessons into practice and when I wasn't: eliminate the words "I'll try" from your vocabulary. If you've committed to getting more exercise, you don't accomplish it by "trying" to walk three times a week. Either you walk or you don't. "I'll try" may lead you to confuse good intentions with life-restoring actions. You can't afford that confusion.

The hope Jesus offers us is that when we put his truths into practice, truly integrate them into our daily lives, we are building lives that will stand strong and secure when the inevitable storms arise. Storms will come, shake your life to its foundations, show you a few leaks you didn't know you had, but your life, built upon doing the truth and not just listening to it, can be strong enough to endure.

Prayer

Lord, I'm hearing many ideas about how to get better, but I must confess I'm not doing very much with them. Like tools locked away in a toolbox, those nuggets of truth won't help me build a better life unless I take them in hand and put them to work. You don't promise me a life without storms, but you do show me the secret of building a life that endures. May I be wise enough to put your truth into practice. Amen.

Truth to Affirm

The truth won't set me free unless I put it into practice.

14

Hold Out Your Withered Hand

Then he said to the man, "Stretch out your hand." So he stretched it out and it was completely restored, just as sound as the other.

Matthew 12:13

In Matthew 12, we meet a man with a withered hand. I'm sure this man did all he could to keep his physical problem out of sight. You couldn't blame him. Many of the people in his day who shared his faith looked at his imperfect hand as a sign of God's judgment for some terrible sin the man or his parents had committed. Some people would not even want this man to be part of their worshiping community because, they believed, only those who were physically whole could belong to God's chosen people. Fearing how others might react, this man hid his crippled hand from as many people as possible. It was his secret problem.

When Jesus came to that man's synagogue one Sabbath day, Jesus wanted to heal him. But before he healed the wounded part of this man's life, he asked him to do something very difficult, something that took great faith and courage. "Then he said to the man, 'Stretch out your hand'" (Matt 12:13).

Before this man could be better, he had to stop hiding his need from Jesus and from the people around him. As I noted earlier (see page 33), a wise man once said, "We are as sick as we are secret." I believe he is right. I'm not advising you to put a bumper sticker on your car that says, "Ask Me about My Depression." I'm not suggesting that you wear a T-shirt that reads, "Kiss me, I'm Bipolar." Your emotional struggles are holy ground, a personal and precious part of who you are. You have the right to ask people to respect your privacy, but before you find healing, you must stop hiding. You need to hold out that hurting part of your heart to Jesus, claim it as part of who you are, and see that he loves you just as you are. And you need to find some very special people whom you trust enough to share your story, your struggles, and your successes. You won't make much progress traveling the treacherous road of emotional illness alone. As Christ leads you to himself and trustworthy helpers, hold out your withered hand.

Prayer

Lord Jesus, you know how hard I work to hide the broken parts of my life. You know how I fear what others may say or do if they learn I struggle with depression. I'm even more afraid of those who would say nothing and walk away. But give me enough faith in you and those to whom you lead me to stop hiding my hurts and give them to those who can help me find healing. I want to be whole. I stand ready to obey your loving command. Amen.

Truth to Affirm

Hiding my hurts makes me sicker, but sharing brings healing.

15

Choose Discipline or Disease

> "Go and tell Hananiah, 'This is what the LORD says:
> You have broken a wooden yoke,
> but in its place you will get a yoke of iron.'"
>
> Jeremiah 28:13

The people of Judah were in the grips of a great enemy. King Nebuchadnezzar and the armies of Babylon had conquered their land, taken away the sacred items from their temple, and carried many of the people far from home. The people needed wise political and religious leadership to know how to live in such difficult times. The prophet Jeremiah walked through Jerusalem with a wooden yoke on his back to symbolize the weight of the challenges his people faced.

Into this scene walks another prophet named Hananiah. He has a very different outlook on the future. He takes the wooden yoke off Jeremiah's back and breaks it, proclaiming that in two years, all the harm the Babylonians have done will be undone. The people and treasure of Judah will soon be returned. His message seems to be, "Just wait. Everything will turn out fine."

After spending time with God, Jeremiah returns to Hananiah and the leaders of his people with another message. The yoke of wood will be replaced with a yoke of iron. If the people do not face the realities of their situation and deal with them wisely, they will face greater hardship. They must live with discipline and a sense of direction, or they will face disaster.

Depression is a great enemy that occupies the sufferer's life. This enemy takes away many precious things: the joy of living, closeness to others, physical wellness, and even faith in God. Depression, like the Babylonians, takes sufferers to a strange place that feels very far from home.

How do you live in the presence of so great an enemy? You must live with discipline. You must embrace your illness and structure your life to survive and overcome the challenge. This kind of discipline is not easy. You could describe it as wearing a yoke, putting yourself in the harness of healing to focus all your strength on the hard work of getting better.

As you make your own decision about living with discipline to overcome depression, your own Hananiah will enter the scene. His message is not one of discipline, but denial: "Just wait a little while and everything will return to normal. You don't need medicine. You don't need a healthier lifestyle. You don't need to examine the ways you think and your attitudes toward life. All that work is embarrassing, expensive, and a terrible waste of energy. All you need is a little more time." This message is very tempting because it takes the sufferer off the hook of personal responsibility, of owning a problem and doing the hard work required to solve it and grow from it. But, as Jeremiah urged his people to see, Hananiah is a liar. Mere waiting won't work. In fact, it invites disaster.

Depression sufferers who refuse to live with the discipline of embracing the reality of the illness and living to overcome it risk deeper bondage to disease. The yoke of iron, more aggressive treatment, relationships beyond repair, even desperate thoughts that become desperate actions often await those who refuse to wear the yoke of healing discipline.

Which prophet will you believe? Will you pretend your enemy of depression will soon go away, or will you live as one who recognizes your enemy's strength and shoulders the challenge of living to overcome it? Will you choose discipline or disease?

Prayer

Father, I don't like to choose when none of the options are easy. But help me to see the road that leads out of this valley and to walk forward on it each day. Help me reject the lie that doing nothing will set me free. My life is worth the work, so help me get going and keep going until freedom returns. Amen.

Truth to Affirm

Living with discipline is better than losing to my disease.

16

Become a True Friend to Yourself

A true friend loves regardless of the situation,
and a real brother exists to share the tough times.

Proverbs 17:17, *The Voice*

A therapist was playing tennis with three of his friends. His partner in this doubles match was not playing well that day. The therapist wasn't bothered by his partner's poor play. Every tennis player has a bad day now and then. What troubled him were the things he heard his friend say to himself when he made a mistake.

How many times can you miss the same shot in the same match?

Why can't you get the stupid ball over the net?

You have no business being on a tennis court!

You are such a loser!

Through most of the match, the therapist didn't respond when he heard his partner say abusive things to himself, but then he reached his limit. He called his friend over to the side and said to him privately, "I'm not sure exactly who you are, but I don't appreciate the way you're treating my friend. He's a wonderful guy and I care a great deal about him if we win this tennis match or not." His self-despising tennis partner stared at the therapist, dumbfounded by what he had heard, and embarrassed to realize that he wasn't being a very good friend to himself.

A depressed person needs empathetic and supportive friends in order to hold on through the dark night of the disease and work through the healing process. No one would argue that point, but what a depressed person may fail to see is that the friend he needs most, humanly speaking, is himself.

Depression can make you your own worst enemy. Your negative feelings can darken your thoughts so much that they become a condemning attack upon yourself. You belittle yourself for falling prey to depression. You condemn yourself for a lack of character, speaking the lie that a strong person, a true Christian, would never feel the way you feel. You overlook every good thing about yourself and magnify every weakness. You rub your nose in every mistake you make, offering it up as evidence of your worthless existence. Does this demeaning diatribe sound familiar to you? How can you convert your worst enemy into your most important friend?

Proverbs teaches us that a true friend loves at all times, no matter what the situation. One who loves as a brother or sister will share your tough times and help you overcome them. Many of us hold ourselves to this high standard when thinking about the friendship we offer other people, but we don't always see that we need to give this same quality of friendship to ourselves.

I've discovered a way to be a better friend to myself. I owe this insight to my wife, Linda. Many times, in the course our marriage, I've shared with her some difficult choice I had to make or problem I needed to solve. I could not see the right and loving thing to do. More than once, she's solved my problem by asking me one particular question: "If one of your best friends brought this situation to you, what would you advise your friend to do?" That simple exercise of getting outside of myself and being a friend to someone I deeply love often parted the clouds of confusion and gave me a clear sense of direction.

Linda's wisdom has given me a powerful tool in becoming a true friend to myself when depression gets a grip on my life. I step outside myself and ask, "What would you say to a beloved friend struggling with this illness? How would you treat your friend? What healing things would you encourage your friend to do? How would you assure that person of your love?" Guided by that exercise, I see more clearly how to be a friend that loves at all times.

What kind of friend are you to yourself? Do you love at all times, even through the long night of depression? In that dark emotional night, you're the one friend you can't do without.

Prayer

Loving Father, I come to You confessing that I've been hateful toward one of Your hurting children. I've beaten that person down with words and attitudes of condemnation. I've kept score of that person's every mistake and closed my eyes to all the good You've place in that life. I've treated One of Your children as hopeless. That person is me. I've failed to be a loving friend to myself. Show me how much I have to gain by answering Your call to befriend myself. As I strive to love You with all I am, teach me to love myself that I may be a true friend to others. Amen.

Truth to Affirm

In the journey through depression, I am the one friend I can't do without.

Part III

Answering *Tough Questions*

"Brace yourself like a man; I will question you, and you shall answer me."

Job 40:7

17

Why Are You Here?

There he went into a cave and spent the night. And the word of the LORD came to him: "What are you doing here, Elijah?"

1 Kings 19:9

Elijah is in a cave, a dark and lonely place. Not long before, he had experienced a great victory, demonstrating the power of the true God on Mount Carmel and leading his people to reject false faith and false prophets. But now Elijah is on the run, fearing for his life. Queen Jezebel, angered by the slaughter of her court-approved prophets, has promised to put Elijah to death. The danger he faces is very real.

But after Elijah's first night in the cave, God asks him a question: "What are you doing here, Elijah?" God doesn't ask questions to learn something he doesn't already know. God asks us questions to reveal something *we* need to know. Along with Jezebel's threats of revenge, Elijah faced another threat—the one that had driven him from Mount Carmel, a place of service, to Mount Horeb, a place of hiding and isolation.

Elijah answers by saying that he is all alone. God's true prophets have been put to death, except for him, and Jezebel will kill him as soon as she finds him. Elijah feels that his recent triumph has turned into a complete defeat and that the mission of his life has ended in failure. This is Elijah's honest confession of how he views his situation. The problem is that his perception is wrong. His view of life that has driven him to hide in a cave needs to be challenged and corrected.

God himself challenges Elijah to see his life differently. God may have used the voice of a friend or mentor or family member to do the same holy work. God tells Elijah that he is not, in fact, alone in standing for true faith. Seven thousand other people have remained faithful to God. Next, God tells Elijah that he has important work to do. Leaders, both political and spiritual, are waiting for his blessing and his guiding influence. Lies keep Elijah alone in his cave. The truth, if he accepts it, will set him free.

Depression and warped perceptions of life conspire against us. An untrue, unhealthy view of life will lead us deeper into the dark cave of isolation and despair. Depression will then, in turn, further distort the way we see ourselves and our lives. The only way to break this downward, darkening spiral is to question the way we see life.

The same lies that kept Elijah in his cave can keep us in ours. Our feeling of isolation can quickly become a self-fulfilling prophecy as we avoid interaction with people and distance ourselves from the very relationships that can sustain us. Believing life's purpose has been lost erodes motivation and meaning. These corrosive perceptions must be corrected if we are to get out of the cave and move forward with our lives.

You are not alone. You can choose to seek contact, conversation, even counsel from people who care. You can reclaim your sense of purpose. You can see that the God who gave you life gave it for a reason. Get busy finding that reason. Volunteer. Help those in need. Support your church. Live like a person on a mission until your sense of purpose is restored.

When you find yourself in a dark and lonely cave, God lovingly asks, "Why are you here?" Answering that question, naming the perceptions of life that have led you into isolation, may be your first step back into life.

Prayer

Yes, Lord, I've hidden in a cave. I feel so alone. I feel no sense of purpose for my life. I, like Elijah, am exhausted and afraid. Come to me, O God, and help me see the sickness and the lies that have led me to this terrible place. Show me the truth about who I am as your child. Guide me to the people and the purpose I need. Lead me out of my cave and back into life. Amen.

Truth to Affirm

Questioning and correcting my perceptions of life are the first steps out of my lonely cave.

18

Do You Want to Get Well?

When Jesus saw him lying there and learned that he had been in this condition for a long time, he asked him, "Do you want to get well?"

John 5:6

On a trip to Jerusalem, Jesus passes by the Pool of Bethesda, a place where many disabled people stay. At the time, people believed that when the waters of that pool were suddenly stirred, it was because an angel had touched them. The waters then had healing power, they believed, for the first person who entered the pool. By the pool, Jesus sees a man who has been waiting by the waters for thirty-eight years. Jesus asks this man what at first appears to be an odd question: "Do you want to get well?"

The disabled man seems to hear Jesus' question as an accusation that he hasn't done all he could to get better, that his condition is somehow his fault. He deflects Jesus' question in a common, human way; he blames his problem on other people. "You see," he says, "the problem is that no one will help me get into the pool at the right time. Everyone is looking out for himself or just doesn't care. If people would be more caring, then I would be well by now."

Having heard the man's explanation for his illness, Jesus calls him to action: "Get up! Pick up your mat and walk" (John 5:8). Regardless of what other people have done or failed to do, Jesus challenges this man to take action to change his own life. Jesus wants him to see that blaming others is an intoxicating way to deal with life's limitations, but it is not a healing way. Getting up and walking is this man's job; no one else can do it for him.

When your life comes to a standstill because of depression and you don't seem to be getting better, your human nature will write a litany of blame, a long list of what others have done to you or failed to do that has left you stuck.

- These are the genes my parents passed on to me.
- My family wasn't affectionate.
- My friends don't ask about my struggles.
- My doctor doesn't know what she's doing.
- I can't stand the side effects of my medication.
- My spouse has given up on me.
- My church friends haven't checked on me.

Every one of these statements may be true. Every one of them may contribute to your sickness and make health tougher to achieve. But, when Jesus comes to us at the place where we're stuck, I believe he challenges us to forget our reasons and rationalizations for why we aren't getting better. He calls us, instead, to take responsibility for our lives, including our struggles, and take action to change for the better.

Standing up is no sure thing when you've been down for a long time. Your first steps will be clumsy. You might fall. But you'll see that your answer is in the steps you exert the effort to take, not what anyone else does for you. Jesus calls us, whenever depression leaves us stuck, to claim the personal power of acting—of taking responsibility for our lives and walking the road toward healing.

Prayer

Lord, I confess that, at times, I've been a blamer. I've explained away my depression by pointing the finger at others and how they've failed me. I don't want to sit by the pool of sickness for thirty-eight years. Help me see that others are ultimately not the issue. I want to hear your call to discover my strength and take steps to reclaim my life. Amen.

Truth to Affirm

No matter what others have done or failed to do, if I want to get better, I must get up and walk.

19

Why Stay Here?

Now there were four men with leprosy at the entrance of the city gate. They said to each other, "Why stay here until we die?"

2 Kings 7:3

The city of Samaria was completely surrounded by the army of the Arameans. Rather than attack the walled city directly at the cost of many casualties, the Arameans lay siege to the city to prevent anyone from coming out or any food from going in. They intended to starve the people of Samaria into submission. Their plan was working. Food was scarce and very expensive. Some people killed and ate their own children. The shadows of death and defeat were dark upon the city and all who were trapped there.

Near the gate of the city sat four lepers. If you think nothing could be worse than starving to death in a besieged city, try being a leper in that same situation. Even among the starving and dying people of Samaria, these men were outcasts because of their illness. But in this story, these four lepers are set apart, not so much by their terrible illness as by a wonderful insight they had into their situation. They looked upon their circumstances—surrounded by a mighty enemy, running out of resources, and facing almost certain death—and asked themselves a question: "Why stay here until we die?" Their present situation offered them no hope. If they continued to hide inside the city walls, they soon would starve. So, they decided, they would take a risk. They would leave the city, go to the Aramean camp, and surrender. If the Arameans accepted their surrender, they would live. If not, they would die. Getting outside the walls of the city at least offered them a chance of survival. As the story unfolds, these four lepers not only live but also find the Aramean camp abandoned, with plentiful resources left behind to feed them and to share with the people of Samaria.

Depression is an enemy that totally surrounds your life. Your emotions, your thoughts, your physical well-being, your hopes and dreams are all trapped in its grip, and you are cut off from the life you used to enjoy. When you find yourself under depression's siege, you have a choice. You can stay in your present situation and starve, or you can take a risk by taking action to reclaim your life.

You can't know for sure what will happen when you leave the seeming security of the walls of your struggle to seek a source of help any more than the four lepers knew what to expect when they entered the Aramean camp. The people to whom you confess your struggle may not know how to respond. Your doctor may not understand. The first medicine may not work. You and a counselor may not connect. Seeking help for depression doesn't come with a guarantee, but it does come with something you'll never find hiding inside your struggle: hope. Some people *will* know how to support you. The right medicine *will* help. A counselor with the right gifts *can* become your faithful guide. Like the lepers from Samaria, you may find more resources than you dreamed possible.

Has depression surrounded your life, trapping you inside an illness that is starving you to death? If so, then ask yourself the life-giving question the four lepers asked long ago: "Why stay here until we die?"

Prayer

My life is surrounded by sickness. I feel trapped and my life is wasting away. God, give me the courage to journey outside my walls and take a chance on getting better. If I do nothing, then nothing will change. Help me do the right thing, the best thing—anything to give healing a chance. Amen.

Truth to Affirm

Don't stay where you're starving. Your life is worth taking a chance.

20

Which Voice Will You Believe?

Then Caleb silenced the people before Moses and said, "We should go up and take possession of the land, for we can certainly do it." But the men who had gone up with him said, "We can't attack those people; they are stronger than we are."

Numbers 13:30-31

Twelve spies had been sent into the land of Canaan to see what kind of life the Hebrews might enjoy there and what strength of resistance they would meet in trying to conquer it. When they returned and reported, all twelve agreed that the land had everything they needed to enjoy a high quality of life. But when the spies reported on the inhabitants of the land whom they would have to defeat to take it, their reports could not have been more different. Ten of the spies reported that the people living in Canaan were too strong to conquer. They were as big as giants, they said, and lived in fortified cities. But two of the spies, Joshua and Caleb, brought a different report. They were confident the Hebrew people could move forward, defeat their enemies, and take possession of the land. Now the question before the people was, "Which voice will we believe?"

When you suffer with depression, you hear competing voices inside you—internal messages that see your life, your worth, and your possibilities very differently. Like the spies who reported on the challenge of conquering Canaan, the messages you hear inside you can give you vastly different views of where you are in your journey.

Give up and die.
It's far too soon to give up.

This medicine isn't helping.
This medicine needs several weeks to make a difference. I may have to try more than one medicine to find the one I need.

No one cares.
I have people in my life who will do anything to help me with my depression.

I'll never get better.
Many people have come out of the valley of depression. I believe I can too.

I don't feel like doing anything right now.
I'm going to do the right thing no matter how I feel.

You can't really belong to God and feel what you feel.
My relationship with God doesn't depend on my feelings, but on God's faithfulness.

The Hebrew people chose the wrong voices to believe. They listened to their fears more than their faith, to the voices of inadequacy and inferiority, not the voices of confidence and capability. Believing the wrong voices cost them dearly. Instead of moving forward into the life God wanted for them, they wandered aimlessly in the wilderness for forty years. They lost a lifetime of opportunity because of the voices they chose to believe.

The voice you choose to believe will decide whether you move forward into the new life God wants for you or needlessly wander in the wilderness of suffering for a long time. The messages of fear and faith are both very real. Your choice of a voice to believe is also very real. The consequences of the choice you make are as large as life. Listen carefully. Choose well.

Prayer

Like the Hebrew people of long ago, I feel, O Lord, that I stand on the threshold of a new life. Entering that life will not be easy or automatic. Strong enemies must be faced and overcome. I hear competing messages inside me: some tremble in terror before the foes I face and the fight required to defeat them; others cheer me on with a firm belief that I can take hold of the life you want for me. Help me to choose the voice of faith, the voice of life, the voice of love. I don't want to waste a day wandering in delay and indecision. Give me the courage to follow the voices that invite me to move forward and claim my new life. Amen.

Truth to Affirm

Faith and fear are always speaking to me. I must choose which voice I will believe and follow.

21

Where Are Those Who Condemn You?

Jesus straightened up and asked her, "Woman, where are they? Has no one condemned you?" "No one, sir," she said. "Then neither do I condemn you," Jesus declared. "Go now and leave your life of sin."

John 8:10-11

Jesus was teaching in the temple courts when the teachers of the law and the Pharisees brought a woman before him, a woman they claimed was caught in the act of adultery. John tells us they didn't care about the woman or her moral failures as much as using her as a way to trap Jesus with a question. They quoted the law stating that a woman caught in adultery should be stoned to death. Then they asked Jesus for his opinion. If, they believed, he said to forgive her sin and not stone her, they could accuse Jesus of breaking the law. If he agreed that she should die, his message of love and grace for sinners would become hollow and hypocritical.

At first, Jesus didn't answer. He bent down and wrote on the ground with his finger. Imagine the tension in the condemning mob and in the heart of the woman as they awaited Jesus' response. Finally, Jesus stood up and gave his answer: "If any one of you is without sin, let him be the first to throw a stone at her" (John 8:7). Then Jesus stooped down again and wrote on the ground.

As his answer had time to sink into the hearts of the mob, each one recognized he was a sinner who, by Jesus' standard, had no right to condemn another person. I imagine the sound of stones hitting the ground as the woman's would-be executioners dropped them and walked away.

Then Jesus asked the woman his words had rescued from the mob, "Woman, where are they? Has no one condemned you?" This may have been the first moment she dared look up and glance around. She saw that none of her condemners would destroy her after Jesus had spoken. With more words of life-giving truth, Jesus freed the woman from her past and called her to create a new kind of future: "Then neither do I condemn you. Go now and leave your life of sin" (John 8:11).

Like the woman in this story, those who struggle with depression can be captured by voices of condemnation. Some are voices from the past, memories of people who seemed to have no love to give us and who, out of their own pain and problems, put us down. Other condemning voices are the fruit of distortion, hearing every suggestion as cruel criticism and every challenge to improve as an accusation of failure. Still other voices are echoes of the pain the sufferer feels, struggling to find an explanation, even a bad one, for why life hurts so badly. These voices wound, cripple, and sometimes kill.

A sad story of condemnation can become a story of liberation when we come into the presence of Jesus. He has the power to confront our condemners and convince them to let us go. He can declare a condemning voice or shaming event from the past to be wrong about you, insisting that you are precious in His sight. He can touch the ears of your heart and help you hear and accept life challenges but not distort them into self-blame. He can touch your mind to change your toxic habit of giving up on yourself because of a moment's mistake.

Before this wonderful change can happen, you must understand that Jesus alone has the right or the power to judge. He also has the authority to set you free. In the presence of his grace and truth, our condemners drop their rocks and walk away.

After Jesus does for us what only he can do, he challenges us to do what we can only do for ourselves: live as free, forgiven people. Just as Jesus told the woman he freed from her condemners to leave her life of sin, when Jesus frees us from our condemning voices, he calls us to change the way we live. We can't believe every voice we hear. In the authority of Christ's love for us, we must challenge the voices that condemn us. We may have to distance ourselves from people who would poison us with their dehumanizing words and attitudes. Jesus frees us from our condemners so we might answer the high calling of living as God's beloved children.

Prayer

I've been dragged around by condemnation long enough. Lord Jesus, I bring myself and all that is in my heart to you. I welcome your truth to overpower the lies that I am worthless, hopeless, and unlovable. But when the rocks of my condemners fall to the ground and they walk away, may I be ready to answer your call to live in a new way, to live as your beloved, redeemed child. Amen.

Truth to Affirm

In the presence of Jesus, my condemners go away.

22

Have You Asked?

You do not have, because you do not ask God.

James 4:2b

I hesitate to ask for the help I need. In my student days, I often sat in class with a question on my mind, hoping a classmate would speak up and ask it. As I grew into adulthood, I noticed I had the tendency to try to solve problems on my own, even when I needed to ask for guidance to find the best solution. I believe my reluctance to ask for what I need contributed to my depression. If you don't ask for the help you need, you may be undermining your emotional health too.

The book of James says plainly that we do not have some of the things we need because we do not ask God. Why don't we? I think the biggest reason some of us don't ask is that we fear the answer we'll receive. Some of us fear that God will respond to our requests by judging or condemning us for our weaknesses. A child resists reaching out to an abusive parent for help, but a child also may not reach out to a parent who isn't abusive. We won't ask God for what we need until we experience the truth that God is love, that God cares about our needs and is eager to be involved in the daily challenges of our lives. I think that same kind of fear keeps us from asking others for help. We are afraid that we'll be judged or rejected for having needs. The people who truly love us won't respond to us that way.

Asking is a healing life skill. Consider how much can be gained in strengthening your willingness to ask.

- Asking acknowledges that you have needs.
- Asking brings you out of hiding.
- Asking reminds you that you need help to overcome some challenges.

- Asking celebrates that you have resources in God and in others.
- Asking affirms that you are worth someone else's interest and involvement.
- Asking breaks you out of loneliness by connecting you to another person.
- Asking exercises hope because you believe your needs can be met, that tomorrow can be better than today.

Jesus says the ones who ask will receive (Matt 7:8). Put the power of that promise to work as you reach out to God and other people to find help and hope.

Prayer

Father, as I offer this prayer to you, I raise my hand to ask for help. Where did I get the idea that I'm supposed to solve problems and overcome challenges all by myself? That bad habit is working against me in a terrible way right now, because I can't find my way out of the dark valley of depression alone. Help me believe that you want to love me and guide me through these tough times. Convince me that I have people in my life who will support me gladly. God who offers help and hope, I'm asking. Amen.

Truth to Affirm

I can ask God and other people for the help I need.

23

Where's Jesus?

Then their eyes were opened and they recognized him, and he disappeared from their sight.

Luke 24:31

When my children were young, we spent hours looking for an imaginary character named Waldo. A series of books titled "Where's Waldo?" kept my children and me staring at and searching pages crowded with characters in hopes of finding that one special guy with the round glasses, stocking hat, and red and white striped shirt. Until you find Waldo in the picture, the scene feels confusing, frustrating, even overwhelming. Once you find Waldo in the scene, you won't soon forget where he is. When you discover where Waldo is, you never see the crazy crowded scene the same way again. You see every other mark on the page in relation to him.

After Jesus rose from the dead, he met two of his followers returning from Jerusalem to their home in Emmaus. As he spoke to them, they poured out their hearts about the earth-shattering disappointment they felt because their teacher and leader had been crucified. They had hoped this amazing man might lead them to deliverance, but the cross, they believed, had proven them wrong. Later, when they reached home, these two discouraged disciples invited their traveling companion to join them for a meal. When Jesus broke the bread and gave thanks for it, they suddenly recognized that Jesus was alive and had been traveling with them all the way home. When they recognized Jesus in the scene of their lives, they never again saw their journey home the same way. Jesus was with them. Finding him changed the meaning of everything that had happened to them.

Depression is a crazy, crowded, confusing scene. Your heart and mind are filled with thoughts, feelings, perceptions, and interpretations of your life that confront you with a puzzle you feel inadequate to solve. The challenge is to find Jesus in your experience of depression. He is there, as he promised always to be with those who trust him. Jesus may seem hidden in the chaos of what you are thinking and feeling. The search to find him is often not easy. But once you find Jesus in the scene of your life, you'll know he's been with you all through your fight with depression. And, like the disciples from Emmaus, once you recognize Jesus on the road you're traveling, you'll never see your struggle the same way again. His love gives you a solid rock on which to stand. His faithfulness assures you that you have the time you need to hurt and heal. The hope he gives awakens your belief that tomorrow can be better than today. Christ's truth can be heard over depression's caustic cacophony of self-condemnation. His grace is daily manna for your starving soul.

Find Jesus in the scene of your struggle and you will find your hope and your future.

Prayer

Lord Jesus, I've been on that road to Emmaus, wondering, like those disappointed disciples, if faith has failed me and you have abandoned me. My head tells me you're in this sad scene of depression with me. Strengthen my heart that I may have the will and patience to seek you and find you. Amen.

Truth to Affirm

When I find Jesus in my depression, I'll never see my struggle the same way again.

Part IV

As You Think *in* Your Heart

For as he thinks in his heart, so is he.

Proverbs 23:7, NKJ

24

Let This Mind Be in You

> Let this mind be in you which was also in Christ Jesus . . . .
>
> Philippians 2:5, KJV

Paul challenges Christians at Philippi to live like Jesus, but he issues his challenge in the form of a powerful image that is, I believe, an important step in overcoming the effects of depression. Paul says to let the mind of Jesus Christ "be in you." As Christians spend time with Jesus through prayer, Bible study, and ministry, we learn more and more about his attitude, his vision of life, his response to people, his way of embracing problems and opportunities. Then, Paul teaches, we can internalize Christ's attitude, seeking to make it our own.

The call to take on the mind of Christ feels like such a lofty goal that, to many of us, the challenge seems overwhelming. I believe Christ helps us take steps toward having his mind by bringing people into our lives who have achieved some degree of Christ-likeness—people who have a healthy, life-affirming, God-honoring way of experiencing life.

One of the ways we can break the grip of depression and how it distorts our thinking is to practice looking at life through the eyes of a friend who possesses some measure of the mind of Christ. I call this person a "thought hero." Answering these questions in writing can bring us in touch with our gifted friend's ways of thinking and feeling and offer us a better way to live.

- What recent experience seemed to demonstrate my depression?
- What did I think and feel?
- What did I do?

- How would my friend think and feel in the same situation?
- What would my friend do?
- What can my friend teach me about living more abundantly?

Stepping inside the mind of Christ or exploring the mind of a healthy friend can teach you new ways to think and act and allow you, in Paul's words, to "be transformed by the renewing of your mind" (Rom 12:2).

Prayer

God, I want to change my mind. I want to break out of the box of depressed thoughts, feelings, and actions. Thank you for the good news that my mind can change, that I can follow Jesus and hide his words and ways in my heart. Thank you for friends who are stronger and healthier than I am right now. May I follow their example of thinking and doing and learn from them the art of more abundant living. Transform my life, O God, by renewing my mind. Amen.

Truth to Affirm

When I change my mind I will change my life.

25

Cope by Giving Thanks

It is good to give thanks to the LORD, to sing praises to your name, O Most High; to declare your steadfast love in the morning, and your faithfulness by night.

Psalm 92:1-2, NRSV

God bless church administrators. They serve as the complaint department more than any other church employee. No one calls them to say, "The temperature was perfect in my classroom on Sunday," or "The light is still shining each night on the church steeple," or "I love the color of the new paint in the hallway." Church administrators receive much more than their fair share of negativity from people.

I once asked a young man who served as a church administrator how he coped with all the negative words and feelings he encountered in his job. I was concerned about both his satisfaction with the job and his health. I didn't worry about him nearly as much after he told me his secret. He said, "In those moments when the challenges of the job really annoy me, I take a step back, take a deep breath, and give thanks."

When you suffer with depression, your mind quickly becomes the complaint department of the universe. You hear every suggestion as a scolding. A challenge offered in love sounds like condemnation. Even when there's nothing negative on your voicemail or in your inbox, your mind creates and repeats self-criticism. What can you do to get your head above these poisonous waters?

I believe my friend discovered a way to put his mind back in balance and restore a healthy view of reality. Like him, when you experience an onslaught of negativity, try taking a step back, taking a deep breath, and giving thanks.

Your first attempts at gratitude in the midst of depression may feel insincere. You may have to say "thank you" many times before you feel it. Thankfulness is like a muscle you must exercise daily to increase its strength and effectiveness. After days or weeks of emotional soreness, your giving thanks will help you see the good in your life and the God who gives every good gift.

Paul challenges us to a lifestyle of gratitude when he writes, ". . . give thanks in all circumstances, for this is God's will for you in Christ Jesus" (1 Thess 5:18). "All circumstances" is big enough to include even the dark days of depression. Counting your blessings in the dark isn't easy, but the Scriptures say it's worth it. In giving thanks, you'll take inventory of the many good things and loving people at work in your life. And you'll see God's fingerprints all over those good things, finding the assurance that even when the valley is dark, you belong to him. You are, now and forever, "in Christ Jesus."

It is good to give thanks.

Prayer

Thank you, God. I don't feel totally sincere in saying that right now, but you know my heart, and you know I'm doing the best I can. Depression has my heart tuned in to the worst of life. I need to tune in a new frequency, a celebration of life's goodness and your grace. For a while, I may count my blessings with little feeling. But I believe that if I keep pumping the handle of gratitude, the waters of joy will flow again. Hasten that day, Lord. Amen.

Truth to Affirm

Giving thanks helps me see the good God is doing.

26

Opening Our Eyes

When the servant of the man of God got up and went out early the next morning, an army with horses and chariots had surrounded the city. "Oh, my lord, what shall we do?" the servant asked. "Don't be afraid," the prophet answered. "Those who are with us are more than those who are with them." And Elisha prayed, "O LORD, open his eyes so he may see." Then the LORD opened the servant's eyes, and he looked and saw the hills full of horses and chariots of fire all around Elisha.

2 Kings 6:15-17

The king of Aram was at war with Israel. Elisha the prophet was providing military intelligence to his king. He used his prophetic gift to give his king advanced warning on the military moves of the Aramean army. The king of Aram, seeing that Israel was always one step ahead of him, gathered his commanders and demanded to know which one of them was spying for Israel. Fearing for their lives, they quickly told their king that Elisha had a God-given gift for knowing their army's next moves. Aram's king decided to silence this spiritually gifted spy. He sent a strong force of soldiers, horses, and chariots at night to surround the city of Dothan and Elisha inside it.

The next morning, Elisha's servant awakened, went outside the city, and saw this great enemy totally surrounding the city. Seeing the strength of the enemy encircling them, the servant cried out to Elisha, "Oh, my lord, what shall we do?" Amazingly, Elisha told his servant not to be afraid, because "those who are with us are more than those who are with them." The servant may have wondered if his master had taken leave of his senses. The servant saw enemies everywhere he looked but found no support for himself, his master, and the other people trapped in Dothan. The servant may have thought Elisha couldn't see the enemy they faced.

The servant was correct in thinking that someone didn't see the situation as it really was, but it wasn't Elisha. It was the servant. He saw the enemy clearly but saw no support—that is, until Elisha offered a prayer for his servant: "O LORD, open his eyes so he may see." When the servant looked out from Dothan again, he saw the hills full of "horses and chariots of fire" sent by God to protect him and Elisha.

Depressed people see enemies clearly. In fact, everyone and everything can feel like a foe when the sickness distorts your perceptions. Depression also blinds the sufferer to the support he or she has in facing, fighting, and overcoming the illness. Depressed eyes need to be opened to see all of reality: the enemy that surrounds you and the no less real helpers you have in the struggle. When depressed eyes are opened, we begin to see doctors who can help us heal, counselors who can guide our journey and help us learn to live more fully, medicines that can keep us above water while we learn to swim, friends who will listen, groups that will support us, books that offer the wisdom of fellow strugglers, people of faith who will pray, and family members who accept us where we are and will love us toward healing.

Before you surrender to the depression that wars *against* you, pray that God will open your eyes to see how much in your life can work *for* you.

Prayer

O Lord, I, like Elisha's servant, have been so blind. I see the depression that surrounds my life and starves me for peace and joy. I know the enemy is real, but I need to see that the allies who will join me in the struggle are just as real. Open my eyes to see the many ways you will work in my life to bring victory and freedom. Open my eyes that I may see. Amen.

Truth to Affirm

The sources of healing working for me are as real and strong as the depression working against me.

27

Let Your Peace Return to You

As you enter the home, give it your greeting.
If the home is deserving, let your peace rest on it;
if it is not, let your peace return to you.

Matthew 10:12-13

In Matthew 10, Jesus is preparing his disciples to go out in small groups to take the good news to many new places. One of the circumstances he prepares them to face is rejection. He knows that as they encounter people and offer them the message of God's saving love, some will not be receptive to them or their words. Jesus knows that being turned away can erode the confidence and well-being of his disciples if they do not know how to manage it. So Jesus gives them instructions on how to live in a world where they will, from time to time, face the pain of rejection.

He begins by teaching them to be open to every opportunity for good things to happen. On their ministry journeys, entering the homes of those who might offer them hospitality and a "home base" from which to serve, they are to "give it their greeting." This means much more than our custom of saying "hello" when we enter a new place. Jesus calls on his followers to offer their blessing, their respect, and their love to the new people they meet. They must not allow the fear of rejection to keep them from sharing themselves and their ministry with those who are open to receiving them. Jesus says that if the new people you meet are receptive, "deserving," of you and the love you offer them, share your gift and make a positive impact on that home.

But what are the disciples to do when the homes they enter, the new people with whom they want to share themselves and their faith, aren't receptive to them? What if people reject them and their message? When hurtful rejection comes, Jesus gives the disciples a simple but profound truth by which to live: "let your peace return to you." Don't let the hurtful behavior of others take away your faith in God, your love for yourself, or your confidence in the goodness of what you have to share. The people you attempt to love will make the decision to receive or reject you. Then, you must make the decision to let your peace return to you and not let anyone take it away.

Reclaiming your peace in the face of rejection is an act of maturity and personal responsibility. When you are hurt, you are right to speak up and call the hurtful behavior the sin that it is. You are right in grieving the wrong that was done and the possibilities that were lost through another person's unloving behavior. But after naming and grieving the wrong others do, you must take responsibility for your attitude and actions toward those who have hurt you. If healing is to happen after hurt, you must consider the healing process as your job.

Unhealed hurt and unresolved rejection is, I believe, a strong source of depression. I have made the mistake of waiting for the one who has hurt me to somehow make things right. I have thought, if only the offender would acknowledge the wrongness of their behavior, offer an apology, and seek to make restitution, then my hurt would end. The terrible weakness in that line of wishful thinking is that I am giving the offender control over my "peace"—over my emotional healing, happiness, and well-being. Confession and the opportunity to forgive are wonderful when they happen, but they don't always happen. When hurt, I must make the decision and claim the responsibility to let my peace return to me. Doing so allows me to say, as I heard one counselor express it, "You hurt me, but you will not control me."

Live a life of love. Offer the gift of yourself and your faith everywhere you go. Many good people will welcome you and be blessed by what you share. Still, rejection will happen. When it does, be ready. Don't let hurt take control of your happiness. Claim the responsibility and the power to seek and find healing regardless of what hurtful people do. Let your peace return to you.

Prayer

Lord, I missed this lesson in preparing for my life journey. My peace has been gone for a long time because I've been waiting for those who hurt me to bring it back to me. Help me see that letting my peace return to me is my choice and my responsibility. This is the only way I can shake the dust of past hurts off my feet and move forward in my journey in freedom and joy. May I claim that power and welcome peace back into my life today. Amen.

Truth to Affirm

When others choose to hurt me,
I must choose to let my peace return to me.

28

Make Every Thought Obedient to Christ

> We use our powerful God-tools for smashing warped philosophies, tearing down barriers erected against the truth of God, fitting every loose thought and emotion and impulse into the structure of life shaped by Christ.
>
> 2 Corinthians 10:5, *The Message*

My father refurbished used vacuum cleaners and resold them to earn extra income for our family. In diagnosing the health of literally hundreds of vacuum cleaner motors, he developed the knack of judging a motor's condition by hearing the sound it made. I remember helping him in his workshop as he went through a box of used motors. Plugging them in, one at a time, he worked like an emergency room triage nurse, giving me quick instructions on how to label each motor for the help it needed. "Good motor." "Bad armature." "Needs new brushes." "Worn-out bearings." "Junk it." Surprisingly, after a time, I developed my own sense of motor sound diagnosis. I found myself seconding the motion on many of dad's electrical diagnoses. He knew when the motor just didn't sound right and needed to be fixed or even trashed.

Every person, but especially those who wrestle with depression, needs to learn to hear and understand the "sound" of his or her own thinking. When depression happens, our thoughts sound different. We could describe the change in many ways: positive to negative, affirming to condemning, peaceful to angry, realistic to distorted. The change is often so gradual we don't recognize it happening. Others may sense it before we do. But when thoughts are broken, they make depression worse.

How do we judge the health of our thoughts? The Apostle Paul offers us the perfect standard. Make every thought obedient to Christ. Judge the rightness of each thought that passes through your mind by asking the right questions:

- Does this sound like Jesus?
- Would Christ agree with what I'm thinking?
- Are my thoughts those of a secure, beloved child of God?
- What do I imagine Jesus would think about this situation?
- How do I need to change my thoughts to make them more like those of Jesus?

My dad's skill in diagnosing motors by what he heard came only with much experience. The same is true for measuring our thoughts by the standard of consistency with the heart of Jesus Christ. Learning Jesus' words and ways by reading and meditating on the Scriptures is key to establishing the internal standard by which we can detect depressed thoughts and work to repair them.

Welcome the help of a trusted friend in diagnosing your thinking. Merely expressing a thought out loud will often give you a new awareness of the soundness or sickness of what you've been repeating internally. Trusting a friend to help you hear, question, and revise your thoughts will unleash the power of a second opinion and a more objective point of view.

Listen to the sound of your own thoughts. If you realize something's not right in what you're hearing, bring your thoughts to Jesus, judge them by his truth, and bring them in harmony with his love.

Prayer

Lord, give me ears to hear my own thoughts. My mind seems very noisy, often sounding as though it's falling apart. I need your healing touch. Teach me your ways, your truth, your spirit so I can recognize thoughts poisoned by depression and make them obedient to you. Amen.

Truth to Affirm

I will make my thoughts true and loving if I make them obedient to Christ.

29

See Your Life Another Way

His disciples asked him, "Rabbi, who sinned, this man or his parents, that he was born blind?" "Neither this man nor his parents sinned," said Jesus, "but this happened so that the work of God might be displayed in his life."

John 9:2-3

The disciples of Jesus had a way of looking at life. They inherited ideas from their families and communities. They had personal experiences that shaped their perceptions. So, when they encountered a man who had been blind from birth, they asked a question that revealed their way of looking at his problem: "Rabbi, who sinned, this man or his parents, that he was born blind?" (John 9:2) Blindness, they believed, was punishment for sin. If this man was blind, either he or his parents had done something wrong and were paying the price for it. The only issue to be settled, as they understood it, was whether this man was being punished for his own sins or had inherited this punishment for his parents' sins.

Jesus said "Neither this man nor his parents sinned," and he gave his disciples a challenge. He urged them to look at this blind man and his struggles in a dramatically different way. Instead of looking for a sinner to blame for the man's blindness, they could see an opportunity for God to work in the man's life to restore his sight and the wholeness of his life. The disciples' way of looking at the blind man did nothing to help him; it only satisfied their desire to know whom to blame. Jesus' way of seeing the blind man's situation, however, opened up the possibility of help and healing. Therefore, to prepare them to continue his loving ministry to the world after his resurrection and ascension, Jesus challenged his followers to see human suffering and need in a different way, a life-giving way.

Just like the disciples of Jesus, each of us has a characteristic way of looking at life. We inherit some of our perceptions from our families, our friends, and our culture. Our personal experiences, good and bad, also shape the way we interpret what we see. People who are prone to depression often view their own struggles in the way the disciples interpreted the blind man's problem. We try to make sense of our pain by blaming ourselves or our families. We condemn ourselves for our weakness, our brokenness, our sickness, and we truly wonder if we are being punished in some way. God could find few punishments more emotionally painful than depression! We may choose to blame our parents for our pain and problems, the dysfunctional system in which we grew up, the roles we played to try to bring balance to the family, the innocence we lost, the love we were denied. The problem with this way of looking at our depression is that it leaves us blind and hopeless.

I believe Jesus challenges us to look at our lives, even our dark seasons of depression, in a different way. Rather than see ourselves as sinners to blame, we can choose to see ourselves as strugglers whom God is ready to bless. The emotional darkness of depression may be an opportunity for God's work to be displayed in our lives.

I've heard counselors claim that merely acknowledging that another interpretation of our lives is possible gives emotional strugglers new hope and energy. Simply asking, "Can I see this another way?" opens our once-blind eyes to see new possibilities of meaning and new steps to take toward healing.

More than one set of eyes was given sight by Jesus that day. The disciples began to see the struggles of others as an opportunity to watch God's love at work. Jesus can open our eyes by teaching us that our old way of seeing our lives is not the only way. We can see even our depression as an opportunity for God to work.

Prayer

Jesus, I confess that the eyes of my mind are as blind as those of the disciples. Too often, I see my struggles as a punishment and wonder who's to blame. Challenge me, again and again, to look at my life in a new way, a way of hope, a way that leads to healing, a way that welcomes God's love to be displayed in my life. Amen.

Truth to Affirm

I can see myself as a struggler needing help, not a sinner to blame.

30

The God of Your Heart

The LORD your God is with you,
he is mighty to save.
He will take great delight in you,
he will quiet you with his love,
he will rejoice over you with singing.

Zephaniah 3:17

The greatest distance I've ever experienced is the vast expanse between my head and my heart. The facts I carry in my brain are sometimes worlds away from my feelings. My ideas about life and my experience of life are sometimes far apart indeed. This gap between mind and heart is not hypocrisy. Hypocrites know who they are but pretend to be someone else to gain the attention or approval of others. This fact-feeling gap, however, is the struggle to be "pure in heart," to achieve consistency and harmony of heart, soul, mind, and strength. This, in the words of the Great Commandment, is the challenge of loving God with all I am.

I believe the distance between the mind and heart is a source of depression. Closing the gap between our expressed beliefs about life and our internal experience of life is a productive path toward healing. In no area of life is this truer than in our experience of God.

For most devoted Christians, the "God of our heads" is very good. "God is love" is one of the first Scriptures many of us learned as children (1 John 4:8). The first song I can remember singing is "Jesus Loves Me." Those of us who've been blessed to be a part of a healthy, faithful church family have heard countless sermons, songs, and stories about God's goodness. Faithful, caring Christians brought the goodness of God to life by the way they cherished us.

Sadly, the "God of our hearts," the God we experience emotionally, can be very different from the God of Sunday school and worship services. God, as we experience him emotionally, can feel like a judgmental God eager to punish and reject. Though the Bible promises no condemnation for those who belong to Christ, our hearts can feel totally condemned. How does this happen?

The God of our hearts is shaped by our families more than our professed faith. As small children, most of us form our first understanding of God by creating a much bigger version of our parents, with both their strengths and weaknesses. Some parents were distant, not affectionate. Some gave rules more readily than love. Other parents changed from day to day due to emotional illness or addiction. The weaknesses of those who raised us can, in some way, give God a bad name.

When our religious beliefs about God and our emotional response to God are at odds with each other, our lives are guided much more by our hearts than our heads. Therefore, we need to undertake the great challenge of healing our hearts and correcting our distorted vision of who God is.

One of the tools I've used to bring my head and heart closer together is to repeat and reflect on Scriptures that celebrate God's love and faithfulness. Zephaniah 3:17 is one of my favorites, for it gives us a glimpse of a God who cherishes us and wants to work in our lives in mighty ways. Here is how I unpack this verse's meaning:

> **The LORD your God is with you**—God is not far away; he is right here amid the joys and struggles of my life. God is not working against me but for me, my health, my faithfulness, and my joy.
>
> **He is mighty to save**—God has great power that he wants to use for my salvation, my deliverance, my wholeness, and my well-being.
>
> **He will take great delight in you**—God does not merely tolerate or accept me. God takes great delight in who I am and how I can love and live for him.
>
> **He will quiet you with his love**—Just as I have seen my children released from fear and quieted by my love, God wants his presence to release me from my fear, the noise in my heart, and give me spiritual peace and quiet.
>
> **He will rejoice over you with singing**—I am familiar with singing songs of worship and praise to and about God. My heart is

stretched by the idea of God singing a joyful song about me. God is glad he created me. He enjoys sharing life with me. In his love for me, God's heart is stirred to song.

A number of the other devotionals in this book offer you Scriptures you can repeat and reflect on to reinforce a healthy, life-giving experience of God. The more your head and heart agree about who God is and how God relates to you, the healthier you can become.

Prayer

God, I realize that I can have the right answers about you and still have the wrong relationship with you. I want the truth of who you are, and who I am as your child, to sink deep into my heart and replace darkness with light, fear with trust, and condemnation with love. Be the God of my head and my heart, I pray. Amen.

Truth to Affirm

To pull my life back together, I need my head and heart to agree about God.

31

When He Came to His Senses

When he came to his senses, he said,
"How many of my father's hired servants have food to spare,
and here I am starving to death!"

Luke 15:17

In what may be the greatest story Jesus ever told, a young man asserts his right to live his life as he chooses. He treats his father as though he were already dead by demanding his inheritance in advance. Then this headstrong son goes to a faraway land, a place miles away from the responsibilities that have so irritated and confined him. What he sadly discovers is that he has also taken himself miles away from his sources of life. When his easy money runs out, he gets so hungry that he accepts one of the worst jobs a young Jewish man from an upstanding family could imagine: feeding pigs.

In the sty, distributing slop that is beginning to look appetizing to him, the prodigal, as we call him, comes to the turning point of the story, the moment when he stops wandering away from life and begins returning to life. The Bible describes that moment with the words, "When he came to his senses . . . ." A moment came when the prodigal realized that his deep hunger wasn't just the result of the price of wine, women, and song; the economic impact of a famine; or the uncaring heart of a farm owner who was more concerned about feeding pigs than feeding his starving employee. The prodigal realized that his hunger came from the way he was living his life. Allow me to paraphrase his new insight: "As long as I stay here, I'll be hungry. I might starve to death. I don't have to live this way. I can get up and go in another direction. I can go where I believe I'll be nourished and happy."

That pigpen revelation put the young man on a journey home, where he found not just a way to survive but also an unexpected welcome, forgiveness, and celebration—all gifts from the amazing grace of his loving father.

I sat in my counselor's office one day, feeling hopelessly stuck in the emotional pigsty of my depression, complaining angrily that the doctor and I couldn't find the right medicine to alleviate my symptoms and help me feel alive again. I, like the faraway son in Jesus' story, was starving for life. Hearing my frustration, my counselor gave me a verbal kick in the seat of the pants that helped me, in the words of the parable, come to my senses. He said, "This is not just about finding the right medicine. This is about how you're living your life." As much as I hated his interrupting my raging rant on the inefficacy of antidepressant medications, he was right. I had made a journey that led me to the stinking, starving place in which I was suffering. The chemical imbalance in my brain was real and needed to be treated, but it was no more real or in need of healing than the thoughts, feelings, habits, and attitudes that had led me so far from home.

I began to realize that day that, at least in part, the way I was living my life had led me to a place of emotional and spiritual starvation. I also realized, like the prodigal son, that I didn't have to stay there. I could move in another direction. I could exchange some life-draining lies for the truth. I could examine some expectations and adjust them to the real world. I could build a lifestyle that supports health instead of straining it. I could change the way I saw myself, my work, my past, and my future. I could plot a new course away from the starvation of the pigpen and toward the abundance of home.

Before you can leave the land of depression, you must come to your senses. You must stop waiting in the pigsty for someone to come along and satisfy your hunger. You must recognize the steps that took you away from the fullness of life, plot your course, and begin your journey home. This struggle is, as my wise counselor said, about how you're living your life.

Prayer

Lord, forgive me for wallowing in the mud of my sickness, waiting for something or someone to take away my hunger for life. Bring me to my senses. Show me the steps I've taken to this faraway place of emptiness and pain. Assure me that you want me to come home to the fullness of life even more than I want it for myself. May this prayer be my first step toward home. Amen.

Truth to Affirm

Healing from depression is not just about finding the right medicine; it's about owning and changing the way I'm living my life.

Part V

Put Them *into* Practice

Whatever you have learned or received or heard from me, or seen in me—put it into practice. And the God of peace will be with you.

Philippians 4:9

32

Swimming in a Muddy River

But Naaman went away angry and said . . . "Are not Abana and Pharpar, the rivers of Damascus, better than any of the waters of Israel? Couldn't I wash in them and be cleansed?" So he turned and went off in a rage. Naaman's servants went to him and said, "My father, if the prophet had told you to do some great thing, would you not have done it? How much more, then, when he tells you, 'Wash and be cleansed'!" So he went down and dipped himself in the Jordan seven times, as the man of God had told him, and his flesh was restored and became clean like that of a young boy.

2 Kings 5:11-14

Naaman was very sick and he knew it. Leprosy was rotting his body away. At the advice of a young Hebrew girl his people had taken into captivity, Naaman sought help from Elisha the prophet. When Naaman arrived at Elisha's home, Elisha didn't come out to see him, but instead sent him instructions to wash himself seven times in the waters of the Jordan River. Naaman became angry not only because, as a man of great military rank and importance, he felt slighted when Elisha didn't greet him personally but also because the Jordan River was muddy and murky. He knew of much cleaner, more inviting rivers in his homeland in which he could treat his illness. Elisha had challenged Naaman to swim in a river he didn't like and wouldn't have chosen for himself.

When you realize how sick you are and seek help with your depression, the people who offer help will probably ask you to swim in some rivers you don't like and wouldn't choose for yourself. They will ask you to do some things you'd rather not do. I didn't want to take medicine because I didn't want to accept the fact that I needed it. I didn't want to be seen in a psychiatrist's waiting room, fearing what people might think and say about me. After all, I was a respected pastor in the community. Like Naaman, I needed to leave my credentials on the riverbank and go swimming. I didn't want to talk about many of the issues that contributed to my sickness. I certainly didn't feel like doing homework. But, like Naaman, with the encouragement of people who loved me and wanted me to be well, I waded into those muddy waters of treatment, learning, and change.

Notice that healing didn't come to Naaman with just one dip in the muddy waters of the Jordan River. As Elisha had directed him, he had to dip himself into the waters seven times. In Scripture, the number seven is often a symbol of completeness. Naaman had to complete the work of being healed. So do you and I. Recovery from depression doesn't come with a few pills or a couple of visits to a doctor or counselor. Healing requires a huge personal investment and the willingness to enter the muddy waters many times in many ways. We must complete the process if we want complete healing.

As Naaman's servant observed, what is too high a price to pay for being well? Remember that insight and wade into the muddy waters again and again in search of your new beginning.

Prayer

Father, I admit that I want healing to happen my way. Help me see that the things I'm comfortable doing haven't helped me the way I need to be helped. My life won't change if my search for healing doesn't take me to new places. Give me the courage and humility to seek and find help where gifted guides point me. May I plunge into the muddy waters so that I may come out one day with the glow of a child. Amen.

Truth to Affirm

The work I'm resisting is the price of the healing I want.

33

Another Way to Win

Therefore put on the full armor of God, so that when the day of evil comes, you may be able to stand your ground, and after you have done everything, to stand.

Ephesians 6:13

Before *Rocky Fights the Russians*, before *Rocky Fights Mr. T*, before *Rocky Fights Again*, there was an Academy Award-winning movie called *Rocky*. *Rocky* is the story of a club fighter, a small-time boxer who, as a publicity stunt, is given the chance to fight the heavyweight world champion, Apollo Creed. Rocky trains with passion to prepare for the fight. He and his trainer, Mickey, devise their best strategy for this chance of a lifetime. The night before the fight, Rocky is as ready as he can possibly be to face his foe. He is too excited to sleep and decides to take a trip to the Spectrum, the arena in Philadelphia where the fight will be held. He looks at the ring. He looks at the banners that picture him and the champion. Then he finds his girlfriend from the pet shop, Adrian, and shares with her a fact that has hit him harder than any boxer's punch—he realizes that he cannot knock out Apollo Creed. He faces a foe he cannot defeat.

We face many enemies we can and should defeat. By God's grace, the guidance of his Word, his empowering Holy Spirit, the encouragement of others, and our will to overcome, there are many victories to be won for the Christian. Do not hear me saying that we should glibly accept life the way it is.

Still, most of us face some foes that we cannot defeat, at least not in the sense of knocking them out once and for all. The question is, once we realize that we face an unbeatable foe, what can we do?

We *can* give up in defeat. We can decide that since we cannot defeat some enemies once and for all, then we must be lacking in faith or may not even be a Christian at all. Many people have condemned themselves like this. Maybe you are one of them. Before you give up because you can't knock out your foe, I want you to know there is another choice you can make. You may not be able to knock out your enemy once and for all, but you can, in your heart, find another way to win. Rocky's decision about his unbeatable foe can show us how.

Rocky Balboa, wrestling with the hard fact that he could not knock out Apollo Creed, did not give up in defeat. He made the decision that there was another way to win. He could experience victory not by knocking the champ out, not by defeating him once and for all, but by going the distance against him. He decided that his victory would be this: to be standing at the end of the fight.

What about us? Is standing at the end of the fight another way to win? Is this another kind of victory for the Christian? I believe it is. Paul describes this kind of victory when he calls Christians at Ephesus to put on the full armor of God. If you read this passage carefully, you'll notice that Paul does not claim that the full armor of God will equip you to defeat every enemy once and for all. His words of victory are "stand" and "stand your ground." Paul says there is a real victory not only in defeating the foes that you are able to defeat once and for all but also in standing to the end against the foes you cannot eliminate.

I've come to realize that depression will always be a part of my life. I'm not depressed all the time, by any means, but the fact that I've faced the hard fists of depression in the past means that I am likely to feel its attack again and again. I, like Rocky Balboa, must prepare myself to stand firm against my foe. I must take care of my body by giving myself nourishment, rest, and recreation that fortify my health. I must learn to recognize the ways my foe can attack me and be prepared to defend the goodness of my life. I have to challenge thoughts that cultivate self-condemnation and despair. I must keep a team of helpers in my life who can be in my corner to help me fight the good fight.

A few people knock out depression and never face it again. Most people must find a different kind of victory, training daily with the desire and determination to stand firm against the onslaughts of the enemy until the final bell sounds, the fight is over, and we know we've stood firm until the end.

Prayer

Lord, when the bell sounds and I realize I must fight another round with depression, I feel so defeated. Open my mind to see another way to win. Show me the victory that comes by preparing myself to face my foe whenever I must and, when each round is over, to stand strong. By your grace, I will stand, and in doing so I will win. Amen.

Truth to Affirm

Going the distance against depression is another way for me to win.

34

Cleansing God's Temple

On reaching Jerusalem, Jesus entered the temple area and began driving out those who were buying and selling there. He overturned the tables of the money changers and the benches of those selling doves, and would not allow anyone to carry merchandise through the temple courts. And as he taught them, he said, "Is it not written: 'My house will be called a house of prayer for all nations'? But you have made it 'a den of robbers.'"

Mark 11:15-17

During the final week of his earthly ministry, Jesus went into the temple at Jerusalem and saw many things that didn't belong there. In the Court of the Gentiles, a place set apart for prayer and worship for all people, a money exchange had moved in to swap all other kinds of money for temple money, the only kind acceptable for temple offerings. Birds and animals were brought in to be sold to worshipers who needed a sacrifice. This part of the temple was nothing like it was supposed to be. So Jesus, with deep conviction and decisive action, drove the money changers, the sacrificial animal sellers, and everything else that didn't belong, out of the temple. Nothing could be there that kept God's temple from fulfilling its holy purpose.

The Scriptures describe a human life as a holy place with a holy purpose, the temple of the Holy Spirit, a place where God's glory is to be displayed. When Jesus walks through the temple of a life in the grip of depression, he may see many things there that don't belong. His saving mission in that life, as it was in the Jerusalem temple, is to cleanse that holy place and set it free to fulfill its holy purpose.

Jesus' cleansing work in the Jerusalem temple was not gentle or subtle. He disrupted the irreverent transactions of the money changers by turning over their tables, scattering money across the floor, and probably sending these people to their knees as they scrambled to gather up every stray coin. He turned over the benches of those selling doves, perhaps sending a few birds flying away to freedom. He stood against those who tried to bring their merchandise through the temple court, stopping the flow of business into a place set apart for God. Jesus made quite a mess of the Court of the Gentiles in order to make it better.

Cleansing the temple of your life will create quite a ruckus too. You'll be confronted by the fact that you've allowed some unholy things to creep into your life and undermine its holy purpose. You may be poisoning your body with food that doesn't give your brain what it needs to be healthy. Your thoughts may constantly condemn God's beloved child. You may have allowed busyness to creep into the place God has set aside for rest and renewal. You may have lost touch with the holy, happy purposes God has for giving you life.

To set your life in order, some tables will be overturned. Some things you've valued will be replaced by more important things. Feathers will fly as Jesus does his work. You may get angry as caring friends and helpers challenge you to reclaim your life. Like the Court of the Gentiles, your life may seem to get worse in the process of making it better. Cleansing God's temple has never been tidy or quiet. But Jesus has decided that you are worth the work. He's ready for you to join him in making your life good again.

Prayer

Lord Jesus, I'm ashamed for you to walk through the temple of my life. It's a noisy, unholy mess. But I believe you come not to condemn me but to cleanse me. Overturn the tables of my misplaced beliefs and values. Drive out anything that doesn't belong in a life dedicated to you. Make my life a place where God's glory can be seen. Amen.

Truth to Affirm

Jesus wants to cleanse the temple of my life and restore it to its holy purpose.

35

A Way of Escape

No temptation has seized you except what is common to man. And God is faithful; he will not let you be tempted beyond what you can bear. But when you are tempted, he will also provide a way out so that you can stand up under it.

1 Corinthians 10:13

Board an airplane, find your seat, stow your carry-on bags overhead, sit down, and soon it will happen. The flight attendant will make a presentation about the safety features of the aircraft. Before the flight begins, you need to know what to do in case of an emergency. You especially need to know the ways to escape, the doors and windows you can use to get out of the airplane quickly if staying inside would endanger your life. Most people don't listen very closely to this safety review, but they might wish they had if a genuine emergency happened.

The journey through depression may include emergency situations. You may face nothing short of life-and-death temptations. You may feel so overwhelmed by emotional pain that you begin to believe ending your life is far better than continuing it. When those moments come, you must claim a great promise and make serious preparation.

God promises that when times of temptation come, he will provide you a way out. God will do his part to protect your life, but you must respond by doing your part. You must be ready to use your means of escape. If you are suffering from depression, you need to choose some people you trust completely, people you can call, night or day, if you feel overwhelmed by the temptation to harm yourself. You need to speak to these people in advance and let them know you want to include them in your critical circle of support. Keep their telephone numbers with you at all times by writing them down and storing them in your wallet or purse and by entering them into the contact list on your phone. You need to be able to call them quickly and easily if an emergency arises.

Choose a safe place where you can go if you feel trapped by your depression. Sometimes a change of surroundings gives a new perspective and relief from destructive thoughts. I have found that a trip to the gym to walk on the treadmill or to a favorite store to walk the aisles and shop for nothing in particular are often helpful. Taking a walk in my neighborhood also offers me a way to escape overwhelming feelings. If none of these places give relief, go to an emergency room. People there can keep you safe until your emotional emergency passes.

Ways of escape don't happen by accident. They are designed into an aircraft to keep passengers and crew safe. Your way of escape won't happen by accident either. But with thoughtful preparation, you can claim God's promise and make use of a way out when you need it—a way to escape dangerous moments and save your life.

Prayer

Lord, I don't want moments of dangerous temptation to come, but, on my journey through this valley of depression, I know they will. Thank you, God, for your promise to provide a way out of those dangerous times. Give me wisdom to find my emergency exits and to use them when danger comes. Amen.

Truth to Affirm

Because depression is dangerous, I must prepare ways of escape.

36

Putting Down Your Rocks

Then Jesus said, "Come to me, all of you who are weary and carry heavy burdens, and I will give you rest."

Matthew 11:28, *NLT*

Feeling powerless, unable to make the changes that will make life better, is both a cause and a symptom of depression. Some aspects of depression feel beyond our power to change: physical symptoms that defy diagnosis or remedy, the search for an effective medication, the daily resistance to life's demands, constant sadness and frustration, to name a few. Healing depression happens more in a Crockpot than a microwave, leaving the sufferer wondering if he can do anything to make it better.

I was feeling defeated by depression when one of my doctors shared an incredibly helpful insight with me. He wanted me to understand that my perception of reality was not entirely clear or accurate. Yes, I had stubborn symptoms that weren't yet changing and might not improve for some time to come. But he wanted me to see that while I had to practice patience in finding healing for some aspects of my illness, I had the power to make other changes that could improve my recovery and enrich the life I'd live after depression. He used the metaphor of a heavy bag of rocks to communicate this lesson clearly and make it stick. He said, "You have a choice to make. You can deal with your depression or you can deal with your depression while carrying a big bag of rocks on your back. Let's work on putting some of them down."

With that image as my guide, I began looking for rocks I was carrying, burdens connected in some way to my depression, but burdens I could put down through making good decisions and practicing some discipline.

If you are dealing with depression, I believe you face that same choice and challenge. You can deal with depression, which is hard enough, or you can deal with depression while carrying some heavy, unnecessary burdens, which is much harder. What are some of the rocks you can put down to lighten the load and hasten your healing? Consider these:

- Resentment over a hurt you've suffered
- A broken relationship that needs to be restored
- A loss you haven't grieved
- An unrealistic and unhealthy expectation you've placed on yourself
- Trying to make or keep someone happy
- The desire for revenge
- A problem you need to face
- Blaming yourself for every bad thing in your life, if not the entire world
- The guilt of an unconfessed sin

The rocks we carry come in many shapes and sizes and with many names. What they all have in common is the burden they add to the uphill climb to health. Do you really want to carry those rocks on your back from now on? Which one(s) can you put down today?

Prayer

Lord, I didn't realize that some of the heaviness of my life is not my disease but my decisions. I've carried some of my rocks so long I hardly notice them, but I can't escape how tired I am and how steep the slope of healing feels to me. Help me to see the rocks I carry. Help me to name them and understand them. Give me the courage to put them down and, as you promise, find rest. Amen.

Truth to Affirm

My journey to healing will be easier if I put down the rocks I'm carrying.

37

Eating for Emotional Health

"Please test your servants for ten days: Give us nothing but vegetables to eat and water to drink. Then compare our appearance with that of the young men who eat the royal food, and treat your servants in accordance with what you see." So he agreed to this and tested them for ten days. At the end of the ten days they looked healthier and better nourished than any of the young men who ate the royal food.

Daniel 1:12-14

The Old Testament story of Daniel begins with an experiment to see what difference food makes in a person's health. Daniel and his friends had been taken away from home as prisoners of the Babylonians, but because of their exceptional abilities, they had been chosen for training to serve in the king's court. As government trainees, they were put on the royal court meal plan of unlimited access to rich food and wine. Honoring the teachings of their faith, Daniel and his friends believed this kind of eating would damage their health and make them less fit to serve the king. They preferred a simpler diet of vegetables and water. So Daniel proposed a test. He and his friends ate healthy food and drank only water for ten days while other trainees ate the rich food and drank wine from the king's table. At the end of the test, Daniel and his friends appeared healthier and better prepared to serve the king.

I am not a trained nutritionist, but I believe these things are true:

- The same bad fats that clog your heart clog your mind.
- Highly processed fast food doesn't give you what your brain needs to be healthy.
- Some foods cause inflammation in your brain that contributes to depression.
- Research has shown that some depression sufferers can be cured by changing their diets.

Many of us have heard the saying, "You are what you eat." That is true emotionally as much as physically. Treat your body as a temple, a holy place where God's Spirit dwells and works. Cherish it and honor it by eating healthy food. In our culture of fast food and highly processed food, you, like Daniel and his friends, will have to go against the eating habits of the crowd in order to make food your ally and not your enemy in your battle with depression. When you choose what you eat wisely, you make a positive difference in your emotional health.

Prayer

Jesus, I often pray that you will be "Lord of all" in my life, but I have seldom thought of serving you in how I eat. I have so much to learn about how food shapes my health physically and emotionally. I think I need to add a new phrase to my mealtime prayer: "Lord, I pray that I am honoring you and cherishing your temple, my body, by what I'm about to eat." Amen.

Truth to Affirm

Eating wisely will strengthen my emotional health.

38

God Anoints Surprising People

This is what the LORD says to his anointed, to Cyrus, whose right hand I take hold of to subdue nations before him and to strip kings of their armor, to open doors before him so that gates will not be shut . . . . For the sake of Jacob my servant, of Israel my chosen, I summon you by name and bestow on you a title of honor, though you do not acknowledge me.

Isaiah 45:1, 4

The Bible is filled with stories of God choosing special servants to do his work, most often to bring deliverance to his people. The names of those God chooses and calls to bring freedom to people read like a spiritual hall of fame: Abraham, Moses, Joshua, Deborah, Gideon, David, Elijah, and many others in the Old Testament, along with Mary, Peter, Stephen, Paul, and Barnabas among God's New Testament leaders. We have no problem embracing these heroes as God's chosen workers.

However, the Old Testament has a surprising addition to this list of God's chosen deliverers: Cyrus, the king of Persia. Cyrus did not embrace the faith of the Hebrew people. He was Israel's political and military enemy. He did not acknowledge the God of Israel as the true and living God. Still, through the prophet Isaiah, God calls Cyrus "his anointed." How could this be? Because God is great enough to use even those who do not acknowledge him to accomplish his work of bringing deliverance and abundant life to those he loves. In God's plan and purpose, a man from outside Israel and far outside the faith has abilities and opportunities God will use to do his saving work.

In your struggle for freedom, your journey through the dark valley of depression, God may choose some special people to lead you forward. Some of them will be no surprise to you: members of your family, close friends, trusted coworkers, ministers in your church. But God sometimes chooses delivers who seem to be far outside the circle of people we know and the faith we believe. God may lead you to a doctor or counselor who doesn't promote himself or herself as a Christian but who has the training, experience, and insight you need to find healing.

I would never have picked Cyrus of Persia as one of God's anointed servants, but God did. God may also place a helper in your life whose qualities seem different from those of the people you're used to but who has the very gifts God wants to use to set you free. Open your heart to the helpers God has anointed to lead you to deliverance.

Prayer

God, you pick some surprising people to do your work. You may want to do that in my struggle with depression. Keep my heart and mind opened to the helpers you might send into my life, people with the abilities I need in order to find healing and a more abundant life. I don't want to miss a Cyrus if you send me one. Amen.

Truth to Affirm

God may use some very surprising people to help me find healing.

Part VI

Strengthen Your Brothers *and* Sisters

. . . we can comfort those in any trouble with the comfort we ourselves have received from God.

2 Corinthians 1:4

39

When You've Returned

"Simon, Simon, look! Satan has asserted the right to sift you all like wheat. However, I have prayed for you that your faith won't fail. When you have returned, strengthen your brothers and sisters."

Luke 22:31-32, CEB

Simon Peter had a habit of making big promises he couldn't keep. He made them sincerely but naively. The night Jesus was betrayed, when he told the disciples they would run away in fear and abandon him, Peter promised he would never turn his back on his Lord. Jesus, knowing what was going to happen, told Peter that he would, in fact, deny knowing his Master three times before the rooster crowed to mark the beginning of another day. Peter would deny Jesus. Peter would know the pain of hearing the rooster crow and remembering what his Master had said. Peter would face the stark reality that he was not nearly as strong or sure as he had once believed.

Jesus' message to Peter that he would fail had within it a great message of hope. He looked beyond Peter's terrible dark night of weakness to the time when he would return to God's family, to his mission, to a new beginning. Jesus told Peter that when he returned, he would have an opportunity to strengthen his brothers and sisters in the faith. Knowing the pain of failure, he could help others who failed. After falling short of his promises, he could encourage others whose lives had fallen short of their sincere but short-sighted words. His new beginning could assure others that they too could get through the dark night of struggle and make a new beginning at the dawning of a new day.

You may not have believed that you would ever enter a dark night of depression. I didn't. I thought I was stronger, smarter, and healthier than that. Still, that dark night came. I suffered and struggled and felt very far from God and from the people I love. Jesus knew I would go through that dark night. He also knew I would come home, and he knew what I could do for others when I returned.

Depression survivors have a powerful opportunity to support and encourage others facing their own dark night of suffering. You can empathize with feelings and experiences that those who haven't faced the darkness can't understand. You can share the wisdom gleaned from your journey. You can stand as a living reminder that depression can be overcome and that a new day awaits those who get through the night of suffering and see the dawn of new beginnings.

I heard someone say that our greatest hurt can become our greatest ministry. Your service to Christ and your impact on the lives of others can be greater than ever when you've returned from the darkness.

Prayer

Like Peter, Lord, I didn't think such a terrible night of struggle would come, but it did. I praise you that you see beyond the darkness to a new day when I can use what pain has taught me to help others find healing. By your grace, I will return, equipped and humbled by my struggles, and prepared to serve you and love others as never before. Amen.

Truth to Affirm

My dark night of depression can prepare me for a new day of strengthening others.

40

Learning the Language of Pain

Your joy is your own; your bitterness is your own.
No one can share them with you.

Proverbs 14:10, GNT

I understand, in a very small way, why veterans so seldom talk about combat experiences. Words just can't do the job. If you haven't lived it, you don't know it. Combat is one of those things that must be experienced to be understood.

Depression is a personal battle that can't adequately be described by words. As one of my friends remarked, "They don't make words like that." This is a lesson we need to learn as we care for people struggling with depression. Reading about depression in a book or studying the symptoms on a web page doesn't mean you understand how a depressed person suffers. In this battle, like combat, if you haven't lived it, you don't know it. The wise helper will heed the advice of James as he says, "My dear brothers and sisters, always be willing to listen and slow to speak" (Jas 1:19). Let's be slow to claim to understand and quick to listen as people try to share something so heavy that words can't bear the weight of conveying it.

While depression sufferers have symptoms in common, the sources and solutions for their pain are as unique as the heart of the person. My depression is like my fingerprints. While the skin of every person's fingertips has lines and rings, my pattern is totally unique. Every person has genes, experiences, perceptions, attitudes, and beliefs, but no one else has my unique configuration of them.

Does the writer of Proverbs mean to say that sharing your depression with others is impossible and shouldn't be attempted? I don't think so. I believe this verse is a loving warning not to underestimate the challenge of speaking and understanding the language of personal pain. The work is tough for the sufferer attempting to share. You may have to learn a new language—the language of thoughts, feelings, memories, and meanings—in order to enter this kind of conversation with people who care. The challenge is equally great for the caring listener. Quieting your mind of assumptions about another person's pain so you can hear a struggler clearly is not easy. Only love can keep our hearts focused on the question, "What's it like to be you?"

Sharing the pain of your depression with others is hard work. Hearing and understanding another person's emotional battle is hard work. We undertake such costly work only because we know that healing is worth the work. Knowing the demands of the task, roll up your sleeves and humbly get started.

Prayer

Lord, forgive me for jumping to the foolish conclusion that I understand another's person's pain, even if we share the same diagnosis. Open my ears and my heart to listen—truly, wholeheartedly listen—so others can begin to express their pain and I can begin to understand. Give me courage to lift the burden of my own pain and move it out into the light of a helper's listening ear. I don't need this task to be easy. I just need to know it's worth it. Amen.

Truth to Affirm

Speaking and understanding the language of depression requires effort and practice.

41

Those Who Hold Up Your Arms

When Moses' hands grew tired, they took a stone and put it under him and he sat on it. Aaron and Hur held his hands up—one on one side, one on the other— so that his hands remained steady till sunset.

Exodus 17:12

On their journey from Egypt to the land of promise, Moses and his people faced a strong enemy, the Amalekites. Moses told Joshua to enlist the men he needed to face and defeat the enemy. Moses, his brother Aaron, and a man named Hur went to the top of the hill to watch the battle unfold and rally the troops to victory. Moses held up his staff, a symbol of God's presence and power, so the troops could see it. As long as Moses held his staff high, the Israelites gained ground against their enemy. But, after a while, Moses' arms grew tired and he lowered his staff. When he did, the Amalekites turned the tide of battle in their favor. What could Moses do? He knew this was a life-or-death battle for him and the people he was called to lead. Still, he was not strong enough to hold his staff above him all day.

Moses had the humility to allow Aaron and Hur to help him play his part in winning the battle. Aaron and Hur found a stone Moses could sit on when he got tired from standing. The two of them added their strength to Moses' strength, holding up his arms when he grew weary. Welcoming the help of his brother and his trusted friend, Moses held his staff high until sunset came, and the battle against the Amalekites was won.

If, on your journey through life, you face the enemy of depression, you will undergo a very demanding battle. The road to victory is not quick or easy. In the thick of the fight, you will find that you do not have the strength you need to win the battle alone. You get tired. You experience discouragement. You feel like giving up. You lower your staff and the enemy gains ground. You know this is a battle for your life, but what can you do when your strength is gone?

You, like Moses, can be realistic enough to know that the battle you face demands more than you alone have to give. You can also follow Moses' example by being humble enough to allow those close to you to add their strength to yours. Others can't do your healing work *for* you, but they can and must do it *with* you. You need people who will hold up your arms until your season of battle with depression is over and the struggle is won.

Who are the Aaron and the Hur you need beside you as you face your battle? You need to be honest enough with your family to let them get close enough to you and your depression to support you. You need a competent physician who knows how medicine can help. You need a counselor or therapist to help you see the big picture of your life and the opportunities you have to grow through your pain. You need some trusted friends who will pray for you and with you. You need people who've fought the battle of depression themselves and will understand you when you share your war stories with them.

This battle is too big to win alone. It's too important to risk defeat. Enlist good people to stand with you and, when you need them, to hold up your arms until the battle is won.

Prayer

Lord, where did I get the idea that I need to face every enemy alone? My prideful attitude has played a part in getting me into the battle I'm fighting right now. Open my eyes to see the reality that I can't defeat depression on my own. Open my eyes to see the gifted, godly people you've placed in my world to lift up my weary arms. Help me put my pride aside and bring them close to share my battle and, one day, my victory. Amen.

Truth to Affirm

To win a battle as big as depression, I need people who will add their strength to mine.

Index of Scripture References

Old Testament

Other available titles from 

#Connect

Reaching Youth Across the Digital Divide

Brian Foreman

Reaching our youth across the digital divide is a struggle for parents, ministers, and other adults who work with Generation Z—today's teenagers. *#Connect* leads readers into the technological landscape, encourages conversations with teenagers, and reminds us all to be the presence of Christ in every facet of our lives. *978-1-57312-693-9 120 pages/pb* ***$13.00***

Atonement in the Apocalypse

An Exposé of the Defeat of Evil

Robert W. Canoy

Revelation calls believers to see themselves through the unique lens of redemptive atonement and to live and model daily that they see themselves in the present moment as redeemed people. Having thus seen themselves, believers likewise are directed to see and to relate to others in this world the very way that God has seen them from eternity.

978-1-57312-946-6 218 pages/pb ***$22.00***

Beginnings

A Reverend and a Rabbi Talk About the Stories of Genesis

Michael Smith and Rami Shapiro

Editor Aaron Herschel Shapiro declares that stories "must be retold—not just repeated, but reinvented, reimagined, and reexperienced" to remain vital in the world. Mike and Rami continue their conversations from the *Mount and Mountain* books, exploring the places where their traditions intersect and diverge, listening to each other as they respond to the stories of Genesis. *978-1-57312-772-1 202 pages/pb* ***$18.00***

Bugles in the Afternoon

Dealing with Discouragement and Disillusionment in Ministry

Judson Edwards

In *Bugles in the Afternoon*, Edwards writes, "My long experience in the church has convinced me that most ministers—both professional and lay—spend time under the juniper tree. Those ministers who have served more than ten years and not been depressed, discouraged, or disillusioned can hold their annual convention in a phone booth."

978-1-57312-865-0 148 pages/pb ***$16.00***

To order call **1-800-747-3016** or visit **www.helwys.com**

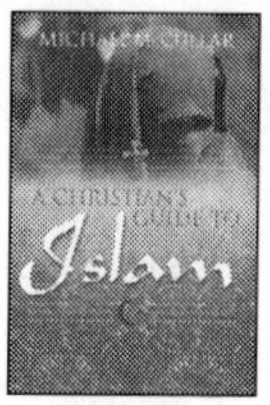

A Christian's Guide to Islam

Michael D. McCullar

A Christian's Guide to Islam provides a brief but accurate guide to Muslim formation, history, structure, beliefs, practices, and goals. It explores to what degree the tenets of Islam have been misinterpreted, corrupted, or abused over the centuries.

978-1-57312-512-3 128 pages/pb **$16.00**

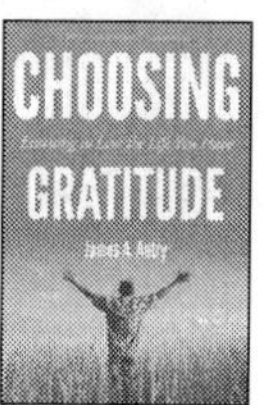

Choosing Gratitude

Learning to Love the Life You Have

James A. Autry

Autry reminds us that gratitude is a choice, a spiritual—not social—process. He suggests that if we cultivate gratitude as a way of being, we may not change the world and its ills, but we can change our response to the world. If we fill our lives with moments of gratitude, we will indeed love the life we have.

978-1-57312-614-4 144 pages/pb **$15.00**

Choosing Gratitude 365 Days a Year

Your Daily Guide to Grateful Living

James A. Autry and Sally J. Pederson

Filled with quotes, poems, and the inspired voices of both Pederson and Autry, in a society consumed by fears of not having "enough"—money, possessions, security, and so on—this book suggests that if we cultivate gratitude as a way of being, we may not change the world and its ills, but we can change our response to the world.

978-1-57312-689-2 210 pages/pb **$18.00**

Countercultural Worship

A Plea to Evangelicals in a Secular Age

Mark G. McKim

Evangelical worship, McKim argues, has drifted far from both its biblical roots and historic origins, leaving evangelicals in danger of becoming mere chaplains to the wider culture, oblivious to the contradictions between what the secular culture says is real and important and what Scripture says is real and important.

978-1-57312-873-5 174 pages/pb **$19.00**

Crisis Ministry: A Handbook

Daniel G. Bagby

Covering more than 25 crisis pastoral care situations, this book provides a brief, practical guide for church leaders and other caregivers responding to stressful situations in the lives of parishioners. It tells how to resource caregiving professionals in the community who can help people in distress.

978-1-57312-370-9 154 pages/pb **$15.00**

Exemplars

Deacons as Servant and Spiritual Leaders

Elizabeth Allen and Daniel Vestal, eds.

Who Do Deacons Need to Be? What Do Deacons Need to Know? What Do Deacons Need to Do? These three questions form the basis for *Exemplars: Deacons as Servant and Spiritual Leaders*. They are designed to encourage robust conversation within diaconates as well as between deacons, clergy, and other laity. *978-1-57312-876-6 128 pages/pb* **$15.00**

The Exile and Beyond (All the Bible series)

Wayne Ballard

The Exile and Beyond brings to life the sacred literature of Israel and Judah that comprises the exilic and postexilic communities of faith. It covers Ezekiel, Isaiah, Haggai, Zechariah, Malachi, 1 & 2 Chronicles, Ezra, Nehemiah, Joel, Jonah, Song of Songs, Esther, and Daniel. *978-1-57312-759-2 196 pages/pb* **$16.00**

Fierce Love

Desperate Measures for Desperate Times

Jeanie Miley

Fierce Love is about learning to see yourself and know yourself as a conduit of love, operating from a full heart instead of trying to find someone to whom you can hook up your emotional hose and fill up your empty heart. *978-1-57312-810-0 276 pages/pb* **$18.00**

Five Hundred Miles

Reflections on Calling and Pilgrimage

Lauren Brewer Bass

Spain's Camino de Santiago, the Way of St. James, has been a cherished pilgrimage path for centuries, visited by countless people searching for healing, solace, purpose, and hope. These stories from her five-hundred-mile-walk is Lauren Brewer Bass's honest look at the often winding, always surprising journey of a calling. *978-1-57312-812-4 142 pages/pb* **$16.00**

A Five-Mile Walk

Exploring Themes in the Experience of Christian Faith and Discipleship

Michael B. Brown

Sometimes the Christian journey is a stroll along quiet shores. Other times it is an uphill climb on narrow, snow-covered mountain paths. Usually, it is simply walking in the direction of wholeness, one step after another, sometimes even two steps forward and one step back.

978-1-57312-852-0 196 pages/pb **$18.00**

Glimpses from State Street

Wayne Ballard

As a collection of devotionals, *Glimpses from State Street* provides a wealth of insights and new ways to consider and develop our fellowship with Christ. It also serves as a window into the relationship between a small town pastor and a welcoming congregation.

978-1-57312-841-4 158 pages/pb **$15.00**

God's Servants, the Prophets

Bryan Bibb

God's Servants, the Prophets covers the Israelite and Judean prophetic literature from the preexilic period. It includes Amos, Hosea, Isaiah, Micah, Zephaniah, Nahum, Habakkuk, Jeremiah, and Obadiah.

978-1-57312-758-5 208 pages/pb **$16.00**

Hermeneutics of Hymnody

A Comprehensive and Integrated Approach to Understanding Hymns

Scotty Gray

Scotty Gray's *Hermeneutics of Hymnody* is a comprehensive and integrated approach to understanding hymns. It is unique in its holistic and interrelated exploration of seven of the broad facets of this most basic forms of Christian literature. A chapter is devoted to each and relates that facet to all of the others.

978-157312-767-7 432 pages/pb **$28.00**

Holy Hilarity

A Funny Study of Genesis

Mark Roncace

In this fun, meaningful, and practical study of Genesis, Mark Roncace brings readers fifty-three short chapters of wit and amusing observations about the biblical stories, followed by five thought-provoking questions for individual reflection or group discussion. Humorous, yet reverent, this refreshing approach to Bible study invites us, whatever our background, to wrestle with the issues in the text and discover the ways those issues intersect our own messy lives. It's seriously entertaining.

978-157312-892-6 230 pages/pb **$17.00**

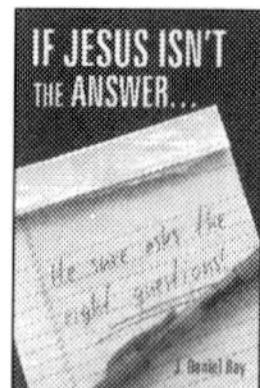

If Jesus Isn't the Answer . . . He Sure Asks the Right Questions!

J. Daniel Day

Taking eleven of Jesus' questions as its core, Day invites readers into their own conversation with Jesus. Equal parts testimony, theological instruction, pastoral counseling, and autobiography, the book is ultimately an invitation to honest Christian discipleship.

978-1-57312-797-4 148 pages/pb **$16.00**

To order call 1-800-747-3016 or visit www.helwys.com

Jonah (Annual Bible Study series)

Reluctant Prophet, Merciful God

Taylor Sandlin

The book of Jonah invites readers to ask important questions about who God is and who God calls us to be in response. Along with the prophet, we ask questions such as What kind of God is the God of Israel? and Who falls within the sphere of God's care? Most importantly, perhaps, we find ourselves asking How will I respond when I discover that God loves the people I love to hate? These sessions invite readers to wrestle with these questions and others like them as we discover God's mercy for both the worst of sinners and the most reluctant of prophets. *Teaching Guide 978-1-57312-910-7 164 pages/pb* ***$14.00***

Study Guide 978-1-57312-911-4 96 pages/pb ***$6.00***

Judaism

A Brief Guide to Faith and Practice

Sharon Pace

Sharon Pace's newest book is a sensitive and comprehensive introduction to Judaism. How does belief in the One God and a universal morality shape the way in which Jews see the world? How does one find meaning in life and the courage to endure suffering? How does one mark joy and forge community ties? *978-1-57312-644-1 144 pages/pb* ***$16.00***

Live the Stories

50 Interactive Children's Sermons

Andrew Noe

Live the Stories provides church leaders a practical guide to teaching children during the worship service through play—and invites the rest of the congregation to join the fun. Noe's lessons allow children to play, laugh, and act out the stories of our faith and turn the sanctuary into a living testimony to what God has done in the past, is doing in the present, and will do in the future. As they learn the stories and grow, our children will develop in their faith. *978-1-57312-943-5 128 pages/pb* ***$14.00***

Loyal Dissenters

Reading Scripture and Talking Freedom with 17th-century English Baptists

Lee Canipe

When Baptists in 17th-century England wanted to talk about freedom, they unfailingly began by reading the Bible—and what they found in Scripture inspired their compelling (and, ultimately, successful) arguments for religious liberty. In an age of widespread anxiety, suspicion, and hostility, these early Baptists refused to worship God in keeping with the king's command. *978-1-57312-872-8 178 pages/pb* ***$19.00***

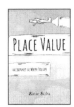

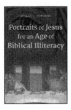

Preaching that Connects

Charles B. Bugg and Alan Redditt

How does the minister stay focused on the holy when the daily demands of the church seem relentless? How do we come to a preaching event with a sense that God is working in us and through us? In *Preaching that Connects*, Charles Bugg and Alan Redditt explore the balancing act of a minister's authority as preacher, sharing what the congregation needs to hear, and the communal role as pastor, listening to God alongside congregants. *978-157312-887-2 128 pages/pb* ***$15.00***

Reading Isaiah (Reading the Old Testament series)

A Literary and Theological Commentary

Hyun Chul Paul Kim

While closely exegeting key issues of each chapter, this commentary also explores interpretive relevance and significance between ancient texts and the modern world. Engaging with theological messages of the book of Isaiah as a unified whole, the commentary will both illuminate and inspire readers to wrestle with its theological implications for today's church and society.

978-1-57312-925-1 352 pages/pb ***$33.00***

Reading Jeremiah (Reading the Old Testament series)

A Literary and Theological Commentary

Corrine Carvalho

Reflecting the ways that communal tragedy permeates communal identity, the book of Jeremiah as literary text embodies the confusion, disorientation, and search for meaning that all such tragedy elicits. Just as the fall of Jerusalem fractured the Judean community and undercut every foundation on which it built its identity, so too the book itself (or more properly, the scroll) jumbles images, genres, and perspectives. *978-1-57312-924-4 186 pages/pb* ***$32.00***

Ruth & Esther (Smyth & Helwys Bible Commentary)

Kandy Queen-Sutherland

Ruth and Esther are the only two women for whom books of the Hebrew Bible are named. This distinction in itself sets the books apart from other biblical texts that bear male names, address the community through its male members, recall the workings of God and human history through a predominately male perspective, and look to the future through male heirs. These books are particularly stories of survival. The story of Ruth focuses on the survival of a family; Esther focuses on the survival of a people. *978-1-57312-891-9 544 pages/hc* ***$60.00***

To order call 1-800-747-3016 or visit www.helwys.com

Sessions with Psalms (Sessions Bible Studies series)

Prayers for All Seasons

Eric and Alicia D. Porterfield

Useful to seminar leaders during preparation and group discussion, as well as in individual Bible study, *Sessions with Psalms* is a ten-session study designed to explore what it looks like for the words of the psalms to become the words of our prayers. Each session is followed by a thought-provoking page of questions. *978-1-57312-768-4 136 pages/pb* ***$14.00***

Sessions with Isaiah (Sessions Bible Studies series)

What to Do When the World Caves In

James M. King

The book of Isaiah begins in the years of national stress when, under various kings, Israel was surrounded by more powerful neighbors and foolishly sought foreign alliances rather than dependence on Yahweh. It continues with the natural result of that unfaithfulness: conquest by the great power in the region, Babylon, and the captivity of many of Israel's best and brightest in that foreign land. The book concludes anticipating their return to the land of promise and strong admonitions about the people's conduct—but we also hear God's reassuring messages of comfort and restoration, offered to all who repent.

978-1-57312-942-8 130 pages/pb ***$14.00***

Stained-Glass Millennials

Rob Lee

We've heard the narrative that millennials are done with the institutional church; they've packed up and left. This book is an alternative to that story and chronicles the journey of millennials who are investing their lives in the institution because they believe in the church's resurrecting power. Through anecdotes and interviews, Rob Lee takes readers on a journey toward God's unfolding future for the church, a beloved institution in desperate need of change. *978-1-57312-926-8 156 pages/pb* ***$16.00***

Star Thrower

A Pastor's Handbook

William Powell Tuck

In *Star Thrower: A Pastor's Handbook*, William Powell Tuck draws on over fifty years of experience to share his perspective on being an effective pastor. He describes techniques for sermon preparation, pastoral care, and church administration, as well as for conducting Communion, funeral, wedding, and baptismal services. He also includes advice for working with laity and church staff, coping with church conflict, and nurturing one's own spiritual and family life. *978-1-57312-889-6 244 pages/pb* ***$15.00***

Tell the Truth, Shame the Devil

Stories about the Challenges of Young Pastors

James Elllis III, ed.

A pastor's life is uniquely difficult. *Tell the Truth, Shame the Devil*, then, is an attempt to expose some of the challenges that young clergy often face. While not exhaustive, this collection of essays is a superbly compelling and diverse introduction to how tough being a pastor under the age of thirty-five can be. *978-1-57312-839-1 198 pages/pb* ***$18.00***

Though the Darkness Gather Round

Devotions about Infertility, Miscarriage, and Infant Loss

Mary Elizabeth Hill Hanchey and Erin McClain, eds.

Much courage is required to weather the long grief of infertility and the sudden grief of miscarriage and infant loss. This collection of devotions by men and women, ministers, chaplains, and lay leaders who can speak of such sorrow, is a much-needed resource and precious gift for families on this journey and the faith communities that walk beside them.

978-1-57312-811-7 180 pages/pb ***$19.00***

Time for Supper

Invitations to Christ's Table

Brett Younger

Some scholars suggest that every meal in literature is a communion scene. Could every meal in the Bible be a communion text? Could every passage be an invitation to God's grace? These meditations on the Lord's Supper help us listen to the myriad of ways God invites us to gratefully, reverently, and joyfully share the cup of Christ. *978-1-57312-720-2 246 pages/pb* ***$18.00***

A True Hope

Jedi Perils and the Way of Jesus

Joshua Hays

Star Wars offers an accessible starting point for considering substantive issues of faith, philosophy, and ethics. In *A True Hope*, Joshua Hays explores some of these challenging ideas through the sayings of the Jedi Masters, examining the ways the worldview of the Jedi is at odds with that of the Bible. *978-1-57312-770-7 186 pages/pb* ***$18.00***

Made in the USA
Lexington, KY
06 August 2018